Maybe It's Just Me!
The Random Thoughts, Opinions, and Reminiscences of a Cranky Old Man

by

Joe Hagy

PITTSBURGH, PENNSYLVANIA 15222

The contents of this work including, but not limited to, the accuracy of events, people, and places depicted; opinions expressed; permission to use previously published materials included; and any advice given or actions advocated are solely the responsibility of the author, who assumes all liability for said work and indemnifies the publisher against any claims stemming from publication of the work.

All Rights Reserved
Copyright © 2011 by Joe Hagy
No part of this book may be reproduced or transmitted in any form or by any means, electronic or mechanical, including photocopying, recording, or by any information storage and retrieval system without permission in writing from the author.

ISBN: 978-1-4349-8325-1
eISBN: 978-1-4349-4572-3
Printed in the United States of America

First Printing

For more information or to order additional books, please contact:
RoseDog Books
701 Smithfield Street
Pittsburgh, Pennsylvania 15222
U.S.A.
1-800-834-1803
www.rosedogbookstore.com

Dedicated to:

My brothers, Jim and Chris, who forced me to use humor as a means of self defense.

Special thanks to:

Judy Hagy for editing and giving me the confidence to keep writing.

CONTENTS

INTRODUCITON..ix
LIBERALS AND CONSERVATIVES 1
FAMILY 4
    FISHING WITH GRANDPA 4
    TIN CAN ALLEY 6
    THE JELLY DONUT 9
WALL STREET 11
    THE GREAT WALL STREET TITTY RIOT OF 1969.............12
KIDS AND PARENTING 14
WOMEN 19
MEN 24
GLOBAL WARMING 25
WHAT IF? 29
RELIGION 31
THE REVERAND AND THE LAWNMOWER..............34
SALES AND GUARANEES..37

TEENAGERS	39
BIRTHDAY PARTIES	40
SPELLING	41
SPORTS	42
MATT SNELL	44
GERMAN MEASLES AND COMIC BOOKS	46
BOAT BUILDING	48
THREE GOLF STORIES	52
THE WORST SHOT EVER	52
FORE MOTHER FUCKERS	53
SIX IRON AUGHTA BOUT DOIT	54
LOTTERIES	56
RACISM AND PREGIDICE	58
SEXUALITY	63
INFLATION	66
DRIVING	67
CHRIS AND ROAD RAGE	68
CUTTING THE CHEESE	69
CATALINA SWIM TEST AND LI'L TOOT	71
KIDS GAMES	74
THE GREAT GEORGE GARBAGEBOATWALK	76
FOOD	82
PSYCHICS	85
HEALTH CARE	86
IMAGINE	88
2001 A SPACE ODYSSEY	90

DANGEROUS PHRASES	91
ALCOHOL	93
BARRED FROM BERMUDA	94
SUMMER JOBS	97
GREAT EASTERN MILLS	97
PETS	100
CHARLIE BIRD	100
VICKEY AND THE FISHERMAN	102
A BOY HIS DOG AND A WELL	103
COUNSELING	104
HIGH SCHOOL	106
CONCERTS	109
SMOKING	111
PORNOGRAPHY	113
WAR	114
NAMES	118
MICKEY MANTLE AND FREDDY DERODA	121
THE COIN COLLECTION	124
I GOT ALL THE SPACEMEN	126
TECHNOLOGY	128
CELEBRITIES	131
POLITICS	134
PHYSICS	137
FUNERALS	138

Introduction

I am a 63 year old man with 4 children, 11-38, and 5 grandchildren, 1-6. I have had two failed marriages and a lackluster career on Wall Street. Since I am retired, my children have requested I put on paper some of my wit and wisdom, mostly as they are worried that being one of the laziest men on earth, I need to do something with my time. I will attempt to do this but cannot promise to deliver in an organized format. I will try, but if a thought hits me, it will be put to print.

I graduated from Lafayette College in 1968 with a 2.4 grade point average. I know that this is not impressive, but I admit to skating through school. Had I truly applied myself I am certain I could have pulled at least a 2.6 average.

How I was ever accepted at such a fine institution is beyond me. With an SAT score barely in 4 figures and a lackluster high school scholastic record, I can only assume it was my prowess on the gridiron that got me in. As captain of my team and a first team selection to the All Area Team, Lafayette thought they were getting a prime defensive tackle. They obviously never read the Currier News introduction to their lineman picks. "It was a lean year for linemen in the area, but these are our All Area picks…." Thanks a lot Currier News; it was also a lean year for local flunky sports writers. Fuck You!! Wow that felt good after 45 years. Anyway, when the Lafayette coach found out he had recruited a 170 pound defensive tackle, he was not too upset that I dropped off the team after one week, and the school was stuck with a lazy, mediocre scholar.

Along with being lazy, I admit to being cranky. I've always been cranky; only recently can I add Old Man.

I am not a mean person. I have friends, and I have a sense of humor, but little things piss me off, and I tend to comment. I am also sometimes politically incorrect but mean no harm. I don't always get the power of words. I used to know African Americans as Negroes, then Blacks, then People of Color! Have these people changed? Why am I still a honkey? And if a person of color is not from America, what do we call him, an African non-American? When did Oriental become Asian? And who cares? Why is it still OK to refer to an Oriental carpet, and not an Asian carpet? Fortunately all the races seem to be mixing, and in a few generations we can all just hate ourselves! What a wonderful World! By the way, is there a better recipe for beautiful children then combining a Black with an Asian?

I'm just saying.

And how about retarded people? What do we call them? It used to be idiots, then slow, then retarded, then "special". Call them what you may, the condition won't change; we just add a few new words with negative connotations! How about Happy people? I've never seen a retarded person who did not seem happy. My son once said he felt sorry for retarded people; it must be so hard. I told him it's not so bad, kind of like being the family pet, only the food is good.

You can feel sorry for the blind, the deaf, or those with other disabilities, and yet these people usually find a way to adapt, so we really should only feel sorry for those who feel sorry for themselves.

Truth is, I like almost everyone I have ever met, and I hate everyone else. That is my introduction.

Disclaimer – The opinions expressed on the following pages are those of an average schmo. They are not supported by any scientific evidence or studies; there has been no research or fact checking. These opinions are intended only for the enjoyment of my audience. Any comments which cause anyone to actually think are an added bonus.

If anyone is prone to being offended please stop reading now. Anyone who continues to read and is offended, get a life and leave me alone. Thank you.

LIBERALS AND CONSERVATIVES

Surprise! As a cranky old man I am a conservative–on most issues anyway. I'm not enamored with abortion, but that ship has sailed. I am sick of every elected official from dog catcher to President being grilled on his position on this subject (from here on out assume his or her whenever I use his so as not to upset the gender police). The law is not going to change; get on with it!

Gay marriage is just dandy, as long as gay divorce is also popular. If it upsets you so much, call it something else. How about gayarrage.

I hesitate to express my conservative positions, as they leave me completely ostracized by many. Liberals find it hard to believe anyone but a caveman or greedy rich bastard can actually express such views. Typical responses: "really, I thought you were kidding", or "oh, you're serious and I thought you were smart". I've had some people just walk away in disgust as obviously no intelligent discourse with this cretin could be possible.

The problem with liberals is they have been totally indoctrinated and refuse to accept any opposing opinions. Today's teachers teach what to think, not how to think. When I was in college you always knew a professor's position; it was opposite of yours. You seldom won an argument as they were just smarter than you. Thus I realized that losing an argument does not necessarily mean you are wrong, just that the other side is probably smarter than you.

Arguing with a liberal is very difficult as most are so darn smart, narrow minded, but smart. Also they are always armed with facts and expert opinions. God I hate facts and experts; they just get in the way of my opinions!

Most experts are unnamed, and when you ask for a source liberals get real upset, as for them, these are accepted opinions not to be challenged. This is also true of facts; they are easy to throw around and when you challenge them you get the rolled eyes. I'm sorry, I just don't trust experts. Experts used to assert that the Earth was flat! All these clowns had to do at night was to stare at space. No TV, no internet porn, no books to speak of, just space. Everything they saw, the moon, the sun, all stars, all planets, everything was ROUND! Still these experts laughed at anyone who thought the Earth was also round! "Really Columbus, you're kidding, right?" "Gee Columbus and I thought you were smart."

Experts are always throwing out "facts" to make a point, and they are always unchallenged.

Years ago I read that the rain forests are being destroyed at a rate of three football fields an hour! Scary stuff! Someone please do the math and challenge this. It is ten years later and we still have rain forests! I'm not in favor of destroying the rain forests, but I am in favor of the truth.

If you stack the national debt in one dollar bills, it would reach the moon! Really, do the bills compress under their weight? This is made up stuff.

If we would only unplug appliances not in use like TVs and DVDs it would save energy the equivalent of taking 20,000 cars off the road! Can someone challenge this one? Are these cars running? What kind of cars? And excuse me, but I'd rather have a larger carbon footprint (don't get me started) than have to change eight blinking clocks every time I wanted to use one of these appliances.

Marijuana leads to stronger drugs. Well, yes, most people who use coke or heroin first used pot. They also first smoked cigarettes, acted up in class, and talked back to their parents. So don't talk back to your parents, because it leads to heroin addiction!

I'm just saying.

When trying to carry on an intelligent conversation with a liberal, try to stay away from the phrase "All's I know is…." This generally lowers any credibility you might have.

It is best to avoid any discussions with Liberals on politics, but try as I do these creatures know how to suck you in. As you try to discuss acceptable subjects such as sports, TV, books, or whatever, out of the blue comes "isn't Bush an idiot?" No response immediately labels you as from the other planet, and ripe for conversion. Bang, you are not only in an argument, but you are trying to prove that Bush is not an idiot (very difficult). No discourse on issues just is Bush an idiot or not? And they have all the pat retorts. Bush graduated from Yale; how can he be an idiot? "Daddy got him through." Bush can fly a jet; how many morons can do that? (By the way it is completely OK to use politically incorrect terms as "moron", "retard" etc. when a liberal describes a conservative. You would think they would not want to insult all retards by the comparison.) "Fly a plane? He was high anyway", and so on and so on.

I graduated from college the same year as George Bush. Trust me, nobody in those days got into Yale solely because of Daddy, and nobody ever graduated because of Daddy; maybe today, but not in 1968. You think it is easy to fly a jet? You fly a jet. Did George try to avoid Viet Nam? EVERYONE tried to avoid Viet Nam in 1968. I'm not saying Bush was a great President; we will never know how great or bad a President was until well after his tenure and George Bush may not have been the best our country had to offer, but can we please start with he is not a moron? Throw me a bone here! If George was a moron, then at least admit you could not put up any candidate who could beat a moron! Is it possible to have an actual intelligent discussion?

Well that's all I have on this for now. My conservative opinions will be spread throughout this rambling.

RT (Random Thought)-Don't you feel sorry for the poor slobs who are actually named Al Bundy? There they were minding their own business when along comes this TV show where this complete nincompoop steals your name. Now, whenever you meet someone you get, "hey, how is Peg?" and "got any good deals on shoes?" You'd think they could sue someone!

FAMILY

When I told my youngest son, Spencer, that I was writing a book, he asked if he was in it. I said of course, so now I have to add this section. I am doing so with very little thought, so let's just see what comes out.

If any non-Hagys happen to be reading this, you are invited to move on to the next section.

Grandma and Grandpa Hagy – My Grandfather was a wonderful man full of life and fun. He had a bit of a ribald sense of humor (for a WASP), and whenever he stepped a little over the line, Grandma brought him back with a sharp "OH MILTON!" Looking back, my Grandmother was a stunning woman, Grandpa, not so much. How he won her over, I don't know. Must have been that Hagy charm!

Fishing With Grandpa

I could tell many Grandma and Grandpa Stories, but my favorite was fishing with Grandpa. I loved to fish with Grandpa and would hang around his house just hoping to go out. After an hour or so of torture, Grandpa would eventually say, "not much to do today, does anyone want to go fishing?"

Usually we fished in the Ocean City, N.J. bay, but one day he decided to go out in the ocean in his 30 foot round bottom and very rocky boat. We caught nothing, and when the wind kicked up to small craft warning speed, we headed back to port. To reach the bay, we had to pass the Ocean City inlet. The Ocean City inlet was very narrow and difficult to navigate in the best conditions. It was not uncommon for a craft to lose control and end up smashed on the rocks which defined the passage.

When we reached the inlet, the swells were coming from all sides and were very high. The boat rocked, was lifted from the stern, and then sent surfing into the next wave, bow almost under, the boat was swinging first left, then right. At ten years old, I was scared stiff (as I would be today), but there was Grandpa swinging the wheel first one way, and then the other yelling "YEEE HA, ride'm cowboy" all the way in. Grandpa was having so much fun that I figured there was nothing to worry about.

Years later after Grandpa was gone, I relayed this story to Grandma. "Oh I know all about it", she said. "He caught Holy Hell from me for that, taking his grandson alone in that kind of weather… He was every bit as scared as you were; he just damn sure was not going to let you know it!"

Loved my Grandma and Grandpa!

Grandma Gus – Grandma Gus was my mother's step mom, I never knew her Mom and Dad. Grandma Gus was so much fun, always crazy and unpredictable, a great Grandmother. I found out later, she WAS CRAZY and unpredictable, and a not so great step-mom! Not my problem. I always had fun with Grandma Gus.

Dad – My Dad might have been the smartest man I've ever known, stern but always fair. He never had to hit his kids (well hardly ever), but had a way of looking at you, disappointment in his eyes if you misbehaved, that would have you wishing for a beating.

Dad was a chemical engineer. When once asked "why did you become a chemical engineer" he relayed this story. "When I applied for acceptance at Penn State, I had a meeting with the Dean. I was ill my junior and senior years of high school, and a bit on the lazy side, so my grades were not very good. The Dean, looking over my transcript, advised that though I might be accepted, being a Pennsylvania resident, I would never get past my freshman year." I then asked him, "What is the most difficult curriculum at this University?"……."And that is why I became a Chemical Engineer!"

Mom – Mom was a great lady, I say was though still alive she has Alzheimer's disease and is not the person I remember. This is a horrible disease; (Kids, if I start to lose it, just put me in a cabin in the woods with a couple of bottles of scotch, a brick of Velveeta, cable TV, and kiss me goodbye!) Mom had a quick and surprising wit (never sure if she knew she was being funny) and always had a philosophical answer to any problem. Thus we seldom brought any problem to her.

When we moved from California to Long Island in 1955, my brothers came home with a lacrosse stick and ball. "What is that?" Mom asked. In those days lacrosse was unknown except on Long Island, and in Baltimore Maryland. "Let me try", Mom said. My brothers explained it was a very difficult sport, but Mom persisted and took the stick, which none of us had come close to obtaining any skill at using. She immediately caught the ball, cradled it like a master, and threw it with pin point accuracy. As we stood watching slack jawed, Mom handed back the stick and simply replied, "I grew up in Baltimore, you know." Mom was always full of surprises!

My brothers – Jim was the oldest, six years my senior. Chris is the middle four years older than I, the baby. When Mom wanted one of us she always called out all three names, the last being the one she wanted to see I.E. "Chris, Joe, Jim" usually meant Jim was in trouble. Mom always called in the same variations "Jim, Chris, Joe", "Chris, Joe, Jim", and "Jim, Joe, Chris".

With the possible exception of my Dad, Jim was the smartest man I've ever known, but he did have a wild streak. If not for the direction of his equally intelligent wife, Judy, (my editor thank you very much) he may have spent his life in the Bahamas baiting fishhooks instead of becoming a physicist, and decorated Captain in the U.S. Navy.

Tin Can Alley

Story about Jim, and brothers: One night when we were living in California, Chris and I were out back playing basketball. I was probably five years old, Chris nine, Jim eleven. Mom and Dad were away for the weekend and we were left with a very inept babysitter.

While shooting hoops, there was a loud screeching of brakes from the highway our house bordered. Jim suddenly leapt from nowhere over our solid six foot fence so common to the Los Angeles area, proceeded to vault the fence on the other side of the yard like Superman, and dashed off to who knows where. Jim was followed by a red faced very angry man with Popeye arms who demanded to know, "Did you guys see where that little bastard went?"

Being five I was about to rat out my brother, but Chris stepped up, pointed in the opposite direction, and said, "He ran off that way". After a futile search, the red faced man returned and grilled us on the "little bastard". Catching the glare from Chris' eye I remained mute while Chris asserted we had never before seen this kid, and he certainly was not from this neighborhood. When the blood started to leave the man's head and refill the rest of his body, he left with the admonition, "If I ever catch the little bastard, I'll kill him".

Minutes later, Jim sheepishly reentered the yard, huffing and puffing, and sweating profusely. Turns out Jim had constructed a string with tin can lids strategically spaced, and attached one end of the string on the other side of the Boulevard. When a car approached, he pulled the string, and the oncoming headlights reflected off the lids scaring the BeJesus out of the driver! I told you Jim was smart, and a little crazy.

Jim is gone now, I did not know him as well as I would have liked growing up, but have many fond memories of long discussions with him later in life.

Chris was always very honest and concerned with what was "right" growing up. No surprise that today he is a Judge. Chris was my tormentor. He was the Lucy to my Charlie Brown.

Wrestling With Chris

One Christmas, Chris returned from College, and I told him I was competing for the HS wrestling team. He immediately challenged me to a match. At this point I was at last bigger and stronger than my tormentor, and quickly had him on his back. Then he was up, on his back again, and up, and so on and so on until we had to stop due to broken furniture. "Jim, Joe, Chris", or "Chris, Jim, Joe" "what are you up to?" Chris simply willed himself not to be beaten by his little brother. He did not talk about this match, but from that day on he went from tormentor to supporter.

Chris also has a bit of a crazy side, (stories I could but won't tell) and sometimes lacks a verbal filter. He was fortunate enough to marry Mary Stewart who keeps him in step. When Chris goes a little over the line in a Grandpa Hagy kind of way, he gets a "Now Chriiss!" a sweet southern version of Grandma's "OH MILTON".

"Pssst, Joe, don't tell the Halloween hose story, or about the birds in Huntington Gardens."

No way Jim, those are in the vault.

"Also don't tell about the cheerleaders and the girl's locker room!"

I won't tell that one ei..........Wait a minute, I never heard that story!"

"Never mind."

My Children

Mary Beth – Mare is my oldest, a bit of a princess, a condition not unknown to very cute little girls who grow up to become beautiful young ladies. A sensitive creature, Mary Beth was always a little bit difficult, but well worth the effort.

When she was ten, as I tucked her into bed one night she said "I love you Daddy", I said, "Well, I love you too, but in three years, we will both be very unhappy with each other." Unfortunately I was right! Teenage girls and Dads are not a good combination. Add to that a divorce and a step-mom from Hell, and times will not be good.

Time heals most wounds, and my daughter, with the help of a good choice for a husband, is now once again Daddy's little girl. To be sure, this Princess has been brought down to Earth with three little ones to keep her grounded, and she is by all accounts a terrific Mom! Job well done Dad, however you did it! Let's give Mom a little credit also, grudgingly.

Michael – Mike was the toughest (middle child, surprise surprise). Everything with Michael was like pulling teeth. Home work done? "Not yet!" Can I get a little help here? "Just a minute." Take a shower, "Took one last week".

I almost threw him through a wall one night because I could not get him to eat one God Damn lima bean! It was at this point I just gave up. Just give him twenty five years and I'm sure he will be OK. He graduated from High School, barely, and wanted to go to Colorado to be a professional skier. He was real good at that! I gave him a car, $50, a hammer, a screw driver, and said "good luck, don't fuck up."

Fifteen years later, after being a no account ski bum, and getting deep in debt, turns out the kid has a great artistic aptitude, and he gets a degree in Graphic Arts. He now holds down a nice job for an Ad agency working 12 hours a day, is doing very well and seems very happy. Once again, nice job Dad. This parenting thing is easy!

Matthew – Matt was easy, called the "golden boy" by his Mom (probably not a great idea for Michael's sake, who was called "Chinese water torture"). His home work was always done, he was an exceptional athlete, never a problem, (there was this little shop lifting incident which almost kept him out of college. You never did THAT to me Mike!), and for the most part raised himself.

He is now a successful phys-ed teacher married to another successful phys-ed teacher with a little boy who will probably be a violin player. He is doing very well, thank you. Another great parenting result. Damn this Dad thing is easy.

Spencer – Then there is Spence-a wonderful little boy who never fails to exceed my expectations. In first grade, the special-ed teacher wanted to put him on the little yellow bus because he could not read. I said, "None of my other three children could read until the middle of first grade. Isn't that what you are supposed to be teaching?" "What's your point?" this expert asked. I said, "When Spencer was ten months old, he was walking. None of the other children I know was walking before twelve months, and yet they all now walk just as well as he does." "What's your point?" she responded.

I (we) basically said let's give it a year before labeling the boy as "special". Sure enough, two years later he is reading books from cover to cover, is on the honor roll (check out my sticker), and is doing just fine.

At age 5 this kid could not kick a soccer ball. I resigned myself to "Ok, he is not an athlete". At age eleven he is the best flag football player in the league and made the baseball travel team. Parents don't put your kids in a box at age five! Relax, let them grow up. At age five you probably sucked at stuff too!

THE JELLY DONUT

One Saturday morning, when Mary Beth was six, I went to the local 7-11 and bought six jelly donuts, one tasty pastry for each member of the family with one left over. I left the special breakfast treats to my delighted children's excitement to go and walk the dog. All during the walk, I was looking forward to relaxing with a cup of coffee and at least one jelly donut. On my return, I found only one donut was left. "Who had two donuts", I inquired? Matt and Mike quickly threw their sibling under the bus. "Mary Beth" they replied. A bit upset at her gluttony I raced upstairs to confront the culprit, Matt and Mike following close behind. Mary Beth was not to be found, no doubt hiding from my expected admonishment.

When I returned to the kitchen, the last of the precious donuts was missing! "Mary Beth" I screamed with rising rage. "Ummfft" came the reply from the laundry room downstairs. I quickly raced downstairs yelling, "Mary Beth, did you take that last donut?" "Nooft" came the muffled response. When I finally encountered the little felon, her face was covered in powdered sugar as she continued to feign innocence.

As angry as I was, with the sight of this pitiful little girl pleading innocence with donut DNA all over her face, it was all I could do to keep from laughing. I am afraid that at the tender age of six the only lesson Mary Beth learned from this incident was the power of cute.

XX's – Just a note on ex-wives, both good ladies with just one problem, apparently me! If my children stay out of jail, stay off drugs and are productive citizens, the XX's deserve some credit.

Matt has advised me that maybe I should steer clear of Irish Catholic women who may have been abused growing up. Good point Matt!

My new girl friend does not seem to fit that profile. Together two years, we have not had a single argument. Is that the way it is supposed to be? Anyway, I'm starting to like not being called a "Fucking Asshole!"

That's all I've got on family, except that growing up all I heard from Mom is what my many cousins were "going to be". One was going to be a great cook, another a great musician. One was going to win medals in the Olympics, etc etc. It is really very hard to compete with what someone is going to be! Know what, all have done just fine (well, I'm trying to be nice), but none ever became what they were going to be! Except Dexter. Guess what Mom, I'm going to be a writer…Well sort of….maybe.

If any of my grandchildren happens to be reading this, Grandpa Joe is sorry for some of the bad words. There was no one around to chide me with an "OH MILTON", or a "now Chriiis"!

WALL STREET

In the spring of 1968 I graduated from college and entered the real world working on Wall Street as a management trainee for Goodbody and Company. Wall Street was in the throes of a "paper crunch". Without computers, and with increased transactions, the street could not keep up with the manual execution, comparison, and delivery of the nine million shares of stock which changed hands every day.

The market opened at 10:30 and trading halted at 2:00. Saturday trading was a thing of the past, and there was a temporary halt in trading on Wednesday, all to provide time for the back office operations to catch up with processing daily transactions.

I commuted from New Jersey, a one hour and twenty minute trip each way: forty minutes on the Central Jersey RR to Newark, twenty minutes on the PATH (still called the Hudson Tubes at the time) to downtown New York, and a twenty minute walk to where I worked at 2 Broadway, near the end of Manhattan Island.

Exiting the "Tubes" I held my breath past the cloud of cement and asbestos dust which was pouring from the still-in-construction twin towers of the World Trade Center. The final leg of my daily journey was against the wind (the wind in the canyons of downtown always blows in one way, directly in your face) past a phalanx of shoeshine stands by Trinity Church, and a multitude of Irish Bars packed at 8:30 in the morning with brokers and clerks downing their first shot and beer of the day.

The Wall Street community was one big Men's club from the highest glass offices to the open rooms of clerical desks packed together row by row. Women workers were in short supply, and the men were 95% white. On the floor of the ultimate Men's Club, The New York Stock Exchange, Women were non-existent, and the men were all white.

A unique feature of the Wall Street community was that workers of the various firms were in constant contact with each other as part of the normal day's business. Communication between firms was required to complete transactions, or to resolve differences in comparing and delivering securities. The result of this close communication between firms was that rumors on "The Street" could spread in minutes, even without e-mail, texting, instant messaging, or tweeting.

It was this Men's club atmosphere and instant communication that created a panic on Wall Street in the summer of 1969 that could only have occurred in this unique environment. I call it the Great Wall Street Titty Riot of 1969.

The Great Wall Street Titty Riot OF 1969

I tried to do some research on this event, but google came up empty. The Wall Street riot of 1970 where construction workers took to the street to bash in the heads of Hippies chanting "One two three four, we don't want your fucking war" made the internet search, but the Titty Riot did not. My recollection may have some errors, but I will let others dig into newspaper microfiche to verify events, if they are so inclined.

In my building on 2 Broadway, there was an employee of a bank who came to work every day at 12:15. I remember her well as I would often see her on the elevator on my way to lunch. She was a big boned woman, not unattractive, but not a beauty. She had nice legs, a slim waist, and HUGE breasts which were accented almost torpedo like by her penchant for very tight fitting sweaters. One could not help but give her a second glance, but no one in the building made a big deal out of her extraordinary shape.

This young lady, Francine Gotlieb was her name as I recall, exited the IRT at Wall Street, right in front of the NYSE every day at 12:05 and did so uneventfully for weeks until one fateful day several exchange clerks on lunch and or smoke break took notice. These clerks casually mentioned the HUGE breasted woman, who exited the IRT everyday at 12:05 like clockwork, to several other exchange workers.

The next day the normal small gathering of exchange clerks outside the IRT exit grew to over one hundred and fifty expectant gawkers. Francine's appearance brought oohs, ahs, whistles and cat calls from the enlightened Wall Street minions as a Horrified Francine hurried past on her way to work.

Word of Francine's unique figure spread, and on day three Francine exited the IRT to the hoots and hollers of over five hundred Wall Street workers. On day four, Wall Street was packed with workers from the NYSE building to 2 Broadway. Cars could not pass, and the unfortunate cars parked on the street had their roofs caved in from the crazed workers who climbed up for a better view of the 12:05 spectacle. Trading came to a halt, and all business activity was suspended for an hour

There were at least 15 to 20 thousand workers crammed on Wall Street, all to see the "chick with the big tits". Ticker tape, time cards and key punch cards floated from Wall Street windows as poor Francine had to be escorted to work by police through the mob and the impromptu "parade".

The Great Wall Street Titty Riot made all the papers and was national news on TV. Francine was offered a spot on the tonight show, and a great deal of money from various strip clubs. Francine wanted none of it. Apparently shy and quite religious, she was humiliated by the attention. The next week Francine was transferred to an uptown branch of the bank where she settled back into obscurity, safe from the Men's Club rowdiness that was Wall Street.

Wall Street returned to its chaotic norm, concerned with the Viet Nam fiasco, stagflation, and a paper crunch which one year later would be the demise of several of the largest firms on the street and come close to bringing the country's financial system to its knees.

I often wonder what became of poor shy Francine whose misfortune was being blessed with a nice figure, and HUGE breasts.

KIDS AND PARENTING

Kids. What's the matter with kids today? Parents, laws and experts!

Here is a list of things that make me cranky:

Strollers – A great convenience in some situations, but I cringe when I see some 3 or 4 year old sitting in a stroller with his knees up to his chin, sucking on a soda and enjoying the ride like King Tut, with Mom acting like a rickshaw driver. Let the kid walk! Give him some damn exercise and take a little more time to get wherever you are going. Why do you think kids are so fat and unathletic? No exercise! The biggest event in the toddler's life is learning to walk, and yet he gets carted around like a sack of groceries.

Car seats – OK, a great safety feature but what expert deemed the seat should face backward the first year of a child's life? My son's head wobbled around like a bobble-head doll when facing backward. No matter how much I fiddled with the seat, they just don't adjust to the correct angle in the backseat. I guess if you are in a frontal accident, backward makes sense, but what expert determined that nobody ever gets rear ended? I've been hit by a car three times in 45 years and all were from the rear.

Baby-on-board signs – What do these people think? That I'm going to drive like an idiot until I see their sign, and then be extra careful? Get over yourself; you have a baby on board, drive slowly and defensively. Don't expect a stupid sign to ward off careless drivers!

Warnings – Every baby related item from car seat to bottle warns that incorrect use **MAY RESULT IN DEATH!** No wonder parents are paranoid.

Cute hats and tee shirts- We get it, your baby is special and real cute! Want to see a hundred snapshots of my grandkids? I didn't think so.

Kid's message on answering machines- Need I say anything? God damn your kid is cute; I just can't get enough.

Baby Talk – We know he can say Ma Ma and Da Da but after 20 minutes of coaxing I don't care. I'll come back in 10 years and carry on a real conversation.

Ever wonder why the word for mother and father is almost the same in every language? OK, the M sound and the F, P or D sounds are the easiest to produce, but why is M always for mother and F, P or D the sound for father? I think that when the baby suckles he goes mmmmmm, but if he latches on to dad, its ptoo, phooey or damn.

Just a thought.

Can we raise our kids sensibly? When a one or two year old gets into something he shouldn't you cannot reason with him. A very calm, "now Johnny give it to Mommy" sounds to the child like "blah bloop padoop". He thinks he is doing good! When a puppy gets on a bitch's nerves or heads for trouble she growls and snaps, and the puppy learns fast. Infants are like puppies, except you can start to teach a puppy at six weeks and it takes at least six months to get through to an infant.

When my kids headed for trouble they got a yell of "EH EH!" followed by a light slap on the wrist. Soon the slap was not needed, and I could stop my kids in their tracks with a simple EH EH! This is the same principle as the doggy shock collar only more humane. To this day I can startle my 30+ year old children with a sharp EH EH. They have no idea why they have that reaction.

Sometimes I just get bored.

Instead of training children, today's parents "baby proof" the house, the car, the yard, and every baby environment. As a result, old farts can't figure out how to open a bottle, a cabinet, lift the toilet seat etc. etc.

Some people think this training is child brutality. I say, "You try to calmly talk your child out of the middle of a road. I'll keep him on the sidewalk with a simple EH EH!"

Helmets for bike riding are a good idea for real riding (while I never knew a kid with a bike-riding head injury when I was growing up, I'll give the experts this one), but a three year old on a trike? Give it a rest. Let's just wrap all children in bubble wrap (warning, incorrect use of bubble wrap **MAY RESULT IN DEATH**) and keep them inside until they're 18! By the way training wheels on bikes NEVER WORK!! Put him on a regular bike when he is ready. Run alongside, give it a push, yell "pedal" and catch him the first 3 times. After that he will be good to go! (Warning, incorrect use of this technique **MAY RESULT IN DEATH!**).

Don't even get me started on "self esteem". OK, too late. Our kids are so full of self esteem that when they finally go to work they ask "where's my office and personal assistant"? Get in your shared cubicle and earn it you little shit!

Where does this come from? How about tee ball and soccer where kids never lose until they're 12. Lose? They don't even keep score! Just a pat on the head, "good job" for every little thing, a juice box and cookie after every game, and a trophy for signing up! Result, the first time anyone keeps score and they lose, the precious darlings cry like babies, because they never learned how to lose.

What about school? In first grade they're put into reading groups, red, yellow and blue. How about "read real good", "read not so good", and "can't read"! You think they don't know?

Then there are grades. Whatever happened to C's D's and F's? Does everyone make the honor roll? From the "Proud Parents of an Honor Roll Student" bumper stickers I see all over, the answer is YES. These apparently replace the "Caution - Baby on Board" signs. Do I have to drive extra carefully when I see these stickers? When I went to school in a class of 30 there would be 3 A's, 5 B's, 14 C's, 5 D's and 3 F's handed out, and you had to earn every damn letter.

What the heck is this Gifted and Talented class in school? At age 6 or 7 who says who is talented? GIFTED? This implies to me gift from GOD! Beethoven was gifted, Einstein was gifted, Albert Pujols is gifted. How are 30 kids out of 250 GIFTED? Let's call it what it is, 6 year olds that read real well! No offense, but from my experience it could also be Gifted and Gay.

I once complained to a parent about this "special" class, and was told "I don't want my child held back by slower children". Maybe, just maybe, I'd like my slow child inspired and pushed by your little genius instead of being put in the "not GIFTED or TALENTED box"! How would they like it if gym separated the kids, and their little precious geniuses learned to balance on one foot while the "Gifted athletes" got to play real games? I don't want your uncoordinated brat holding back my future Hall Of Famer!

If your child is truly gifted, no other child could hold him back! If you locked a six year old Beethoven in a closet with 16 bottles and a gallon of water he would come out with a symphony!

I really hate the "Take your kid to work day". It started as "take your daughter to work "as some expert determined that little girls' self esteem was lower than little boys'. I say why not just round up the little boys to assembly, and announce "YOU SUCK". That will even out the self esteem gender gap.

Now these little brats come to work where secretaries and assistants have to cater to them all day, and work overtime the next day to catch up on their real jobs. Once again, gather them all up in the assembly hall and tell them, "Mommy and Daddy go to work every day, bust their asses, and take crap from customers and bosses, so you can wear designer clothes and eat gourmet peanut butter; now go back to class!"

By the way since when did peanut butter become a killer? How is this something new? Kids are allergic to everything now because they are so protected! Send them out to roll in the dirt at an early age and they will be just fine. Puppies eat poop for Christ's sake!

I just read an article by some expert on the six reasons children throw tantrums, and how to avoid them. This expert relates that sometimes children are tired, or hungry (no DUH), so make sure your child is rested and fed before any activity. How many years of school did this guy go through to learn what is deep in the DNA of every mother? Always have a snack at hand, an apple or some other fruit. Yeah, that's what every cranky child wants, an apple! Carry a watch and show the little darling just how much time before we can end the activity. If your child can tell time and is still throwing tantrums, you already screwed up somewhere! If the child does not want to leave the playground, try telling him "just five minutes, and then when we go you can have some ice cream". He left out getting on your knees and exhorting "Please, pretty please, do it for Mommy ".

Really, this is a little kid. TAKE CHARGE! Do a Cesar Millan, and be the pack leader. My son Spencer threw a tantrum one time, over I don't remember what. He started kicking, screaming, and rolling on the kitchen floor. His mother and I totally ignored it. We went about our business, never acknowledging the ruckus, stepped over him, left the room, and returned again. At one point one of us looked at him and said "wrong parents!" After about ten minutes he stopped, and he never threw a tantrum again.

When your child wants something and you don't think it is appropriate, explain your reason, and stand firm. "Because I said so" is not really productive. Don't get in the habit of saying no to everything. Every once in a while give it a "sure, why not?" Basically parents, take charge and go with your gut. Readers Digest ten point expert advice is nice reading, but every parent is different, and you need to parent based on your own disposition and personality. What works for one will not work for everyone, but DO be the boss of him. "You're not the boss of me!" Oh yes I am!!

I know parents, very nice people. Both the husband and wife are very intelligent, and so is their son. They were desperate to toilet train their son before he went to pre-school. "Please, Billy, if you poop in the pot we will give you five dollars." They thought this would work. Kid was smart, he was holding out for more! One day of pre-school with thirty kids ready to taunt, and surprise, Billy knew when and where to poop.

Maybe it's just me

RT - random thought: If I could do anything I wanted to Paris Hilton, I would slap her! Guess that makes me a cranky old man.

WOMEN

With two failed marriages, obviously I don't know much on this subject, but I do have opinions!

First, I am absolutely convinced by personal observation (contrary to many experts), that women and men are different. Women are smaller, physically weaker, run slower, and I am positive are built different than Men. Originally this all worked out quite nicely. Big strong fast Man killed animals for food, plowed fields, and protected the home, while small frail slow Woman bore children, nurtured the children, and made things nice at home for their provider and protector, Man. For those men who did not provide or protect well, families did not survive. Thus Woman invented nagging, and Man was sure to provide. Originally, Man and Woman only lived for about 30 years, and all was well.

Then with extended life expectancy, the formula did not work. Man and Woman found coexisting for over 10 years to be difficult, and got on each other's nerves (something not possible when all thought was on "how the heck do we survive tomorrow?"), and Woman had nothing to do after the children grew up. The new age brought a new issue never before experienced, boredom.

Next thing is Woman demanded to be treated as equals! They could provide for themselves quite nicely at the Supermarket, and were protected by Police. Man became a burden. He was off to work in the morning, home at night, and money was deposited in the bank every two weeks. Woman could do that!

Thus nagging became an outlet for frustration! Help with the kids, help clean up, "I'm exhausted, and all you do is come home and plop in front of the TV, you lazy bum!" In the good old days when duties were well defined, Woman saw her man sweating and tired from hunting and plowing, and did everything possible to make him comfortable so he could get up and do it all over again the next day so they could survive. When Woman no longer saw her Man working, she lost appreciation for what he did, and if she does not see you working, it does not count, and a day of rest became a day of yard work, and babysitting.

Soon Woman learned they could do what Man could do and Woman's Liberation was invented. With lines of responsibilities crossed, worlds collided! Man was no longer needed for survival, and was forced to do things he was not designed to do in order to survive. Changing diapers, washing dishes, vacuuming, and folding clothes became necessary chores which were never done correctly! And then nagging became an art form!

The blurring of responsibilities is such a problem that some people are blowing up buildings and people to prevent this change from infiltrating their culture. The cause of terrorism today has nothing to do with oil or religion; it is the underlying fear of westernization of their Women. The end of terrorism will come when these Women start to get well timed headaches, and learn to nag! If they don't see Achmed blow up the building, what the fuck did he do all day?

Women are angry, and who can blame them? Their plumbing is very inconvenient. They can't pull over on the highway to relieve themselves, they miss the third quarters of football games standing in line at the ladies room, they never enjoyed the thrill of spelling their name in the snow, and to further exacerbate the problem they are reminded very unpleasantly of their condition every month, and nagging turns to rage!

Now I do love women but why can't they learn how to buy stuff? A man will approach the cashier with a bill in hand, give it over to the cashier, then move to the right to receive his change, jam it in his pocket, say thank you and leave.

Women approach with pocketbook in hand waiting for their purchase total. When the total cost is revealed, then and only then will they open up the pocket book, remove their purse and root around for the exact amount which will return to them the least amount of change. Then without moving they carefully put away the bills and change, snap their purse shut, put it in the pocketbook, strap that shut, and finally leave without saying thank you. Women, please MOVE TO THE RIGHT!

Women always ask men about what they are wearing, "Does this look ok?" Why I don't know. First of all, they are only worried about what other women and gay men think, and we don't have a clue, secondly no man in his right mind would say what he really thinks anyway. My teenage daughter once asked me, "Daddy does this outfit look too slutty?" –a question every father dreams to hear, and I told her "no sweetheart, you look just slutty enough." Two rules: women-don't ask, men-don't tell.

There is the old joke about men never asking for directions. It's true, but women will ask any pimple-faced teen pumping gas, and actually try to follow "well you go straight about three lights, then turn left at the gas station, go about three blocks and turn right at the fast food restaurant, then about three miles to your right and you can't miss it." First off, I don't want to hear "about" when following directions; secondly there is a gas station or fast food restaurant on every corner, and last, for the same reason men won't ask for directions, they won't admit they don't know when you ask them!

It seems like every year the TV news does a report on the cost of women's clothes and dry cleaning. The indignant reporter demonstrates that comparable apparel costs more for women than men, and the obvious conclusion is discrimination against women.

First off if a company could make a profit at a lower price and increased sales they would. Companies don't discriminate against customers; they try to maximize profits. Second, I submit that there are no comparable clothes for men and women. Even a simple blouse has a million variations of collar sizes and designs, pleats, and colors. Men's shirts are all virtually the same in design and color selection. 90% are white or a shade of blue. It is obviously cheaper to mass produce an item than to manufacture a vast variety of the same product. Third, have you ever heard of a man buying an outfit to wear to a specific function only to return it the next week and expect a full refund? I rest my case.

As to the dry cleaner story, women are simply more demanding. Men pay the cleaner, count the shirts, say thank you and leave. Women go thru every item with a fine tooth comb, and will complain about any perceived flaw, some which were present when the item was dropped off. Sorry women. It is fine to be demanding, but it does cost more.

Every year the newspapers also do a story on the "real value" of stay-at-home mothers. Now I am completely in favor of stay-at-home moms or dads and respect the sacrifice many women make to parent their children full time, and nobody does it better than mom, but is this story fair?

This yearly article ascribes to moms a prorated salary for each and every function they provide, and then calculates the cost to hire out these duties. Housekeeper @$20 an hour, clerk $20, child care specialist $30, psychologist $50, cook $35, accountant $100, and CEO $300 per hour, chauffer, etc etc all at 15 hours per day, seven days a week. Every year when this report comes out, poor schlub husbands throughout the country come home sweaty and tired, and have this report shoved in their face with the demand "You owe me $250,000 a year!".

Pahleese! We appreciate all you do, and no one does it better, but 15 hours a day, seven days a week? Does the man do nothing when he comes home, and on weekends? I know I did. Maybe he did not in the 50's, but he does today. I know that man cannot perform these tasks as well as women, but HELL, go get a full time job as CEO, bring home $500,000 and I can do pretty well with plenty of money left over to hire out what I can't handle!

IF women want to dress to please man, they should take a lesson from Hookers-Platform shoes with six inch stiletto heels, skirt hiked up to their butt, and cleavage spilling out. When one of these creatures enters a room man inevitably gets an elbow nudge,

"Look at that. Isn't that disgusting?"

"What....oh, that, I did not even notice that....why that is disgusting!" "Excuse me while I adjust my shorts!!"

Women also have language skills that men can never decipher. At a young age, boys are getting in trouble at school for talking in class, while the girls carry on a complete conversation at opposite sides of the room using sign language and lip reading, and never get caught.

Women communicate with hand or facial gestures, and voice intonations which go completely over man's head. I have stood with my wife while she carried on a perfectly delightful conversation with another woman, on whose departure she turns to me and says, "Do you believe her? What a Bitch!" I just nod my head in agreement......haven't got a clue.

Women are not all bad; man just needs to learn to adapt to the new world. Man is perfectly happy with his own home, sheets for curtains, book cases of bricks and planks, dishes in the sink, change of clothes on the floor, a beer in hand, and a game on TV, and then he gets married. Why, he is not sure, but all his friends did it and suddenly he has no friends. And so he marries, and sheets become frilly, furniture is IKEA, dishes are clean and put away, clothes are clean and in a drawer and he sees "this is good". Blow up dolls are replaced by flesh and warmth and "this is very good". A beer in hand and a game on TV become a luxury earned by yard chores, compliments, and good behavior, and all is well worth the effort.

Without women, pennies would be obsolete. Because they have no pockets, women actually use pennies. Supposedly inept at math, any woman immediately knows just how much change to pay in order to reduce the number of pennies in her purse. If something costs 98 cents, a woman will pay $1.03 and get back a nickel. A man will pay $1.00 and get back 2 pennies which end up in a gallon water jug, forever out of circulation. Without women, all prices would be rounded up to increments of a nickel and inflation would be rampant.

Without women there would be no fashion or cosmetic industry, and the economy would be in shambles. Men would all simply wear the same shirts and pants and smell bad. The only real fashion for men is the tie, a completely useless garment whose sole purpose is for a woman to criticize if they did not themselves pick it out.

Without women there would be no home, there would be no countries, no borders, no one, or nothing to protect. Man would be nomadic, wandering around, killing animals, picking berries and high fiving other men who also had no woman to protect. There would be no wars, and another industry destroyed.

I'm just saying.

RT - I know profiling is wrong, but for the time being, just to be safe if given the choice between Granny and the guy with one eyebrow and a strap on beard, let's give the later a cavity search!

Maybe it's just me.

MEN

This is easy. Men are dirty, smelly, hairy creatures. I just do not understand gay men, but lesbianism makes perfect sense to me!

RT - If you are older than 18 living in this country and reading this you have a better life than 99.8% of every human ever born. Even the Pharaohs and kings of olden days didn't have decent toilet paper, salt was a luxury, slaves with huge feathers were not nearly as good as air conditioning, everything smelled, no one cleaned up after the horses, and TV probably only had 4 channels.

GLOBAL WARMING

Experts again! Now I'm in favor of most of the goals of the global warming alarmist, less emission, cleaner air, and all that good stuff, but I don't believe the hype and the politicalization of a theory. That's right; it's just a theory which many experts, at great risk of being labeled nut cases disagree with. First off who are these experts? Climatologists. Sorry, but I've met many very very smart people, and never met one who said "I want to be a climatologist!" Climatologists are to scientists what podiatrists are to heart surgeons. Smart, but not the cream of the crop.

They are trying to explain why the Earth has increased in temperature 1 friggin degree in the last 100 years. First, I think it is amazing that the Earth's temperature has only changed 1 degree in 100 years. If it was exactly the same, it would be a miracle. Second, how do we know this 1 degree is fact? Is there not a plus or minus factor in this measurement? Political polls have a plus or minus factor of 5 %. Are measurements of the Earth's temperature more accurate? Is there no room for error?

Who is taking these temperatures all over the globe for 100 years? Is it possible some idiot reported temperatures in Fahrenheit instead of Celsius? There were no computers for 80 of those years. Was anyone double checking the numbers? Where are these temperatures taken? Was one area near a forest in 1919 and it is now near The Garden State Parkway?

I once drove through the Bronx, and watched the temperature change 10 degrees as we went through the city area. There are so many variables it is ridiculous! Is anyone taking temperatures in the middle of the Atlantic? One god damn degree for goodness sake!

It just feels real good to save the Earth. School children are all being taught this theory as fact! When you question this theory you get "you're kidding, right?" Let's all just follow the experts into the sea, no room for discussion. You can't question the experts! Let's not take the chance that the experts are wrong. It may, be too late.

Well say it is correct. What can we do besides a lot of feel good crap. Turn off lights, drive 55 walk to work etc. etc., all negated by one smuck driving his cigarette boat 60 knots to go nowhere. And who is going to profit from global warming legislation, carbon offsets and such? The rich asshole driving the cigarette boat or flying his Lear Jet to summer at the Cape!

Computer models show......Pahleese! How do they factor in all variables? Does the Earth's axis never vary even a little? How is that measured? Does the Sun emit the exact amount of heat every year? Wow, if it does, how does anybody not believe in God?

I want to know how the Sun does not burn out! Ask that question and watch the eyes roll, and yet I've never met anyone who can give me an answer! No energy source can last forever, or not deplete a little, but we don't worry about that because there is not a damn thing we can do about it. Maybe we should add to greenhouse gasses to counteract the obvious decreasing heat from the sun.

The Earth rotates on its axis exactly once every 24 hours. We base our units of time on this fact, and in thousands of years it has never let us down. Does that astound only me? The Earth circles the Sun exactly once every 365.25 days. Never any faster or slower, for as long as man has followed this event it has remained exactly once every 365.25 days. Any faster or slower and after a thousand years, January would become April. If you spit on a thrown baseball it will spin at a different rate, yet we have erected huge buildings, dug huge tunnels, excavated for coal, oil and minerals all changing the shape of Earth and still it rotates one time every 24 hours. Exactly 24 hours, no deviation by even one second for at least 2000+years. We can predict high and low tides years ahead. EXACTLY. No deviation! This requires exact rotation of the Earth on its axis, exact position in its journey around the Sun and exact movement of the Moon around the Earth for thousands of years. Yawn, ho hum, no biggie, so let's get on with controlling the climate. Man can do anything.

The problem is man is so guilty about ruining the ecology; we are upsetting the natural ways of the ecology. Here is a thought; we are all part of the ecology, all part of the natural way of things, and only man can make conscious decisions as to his actions.

If we want to wipe out the snail darter, we can. We don't, but we can. Apparently we like snail darters, and believe if they were wiped off the Earth, other fish would die, birds which live off the fish would die, etc. etc. and the world as we know it would end.

Does the great white shark worry about the seal population? Hell, they will eat as many as possible. Does anyone miss the Tyrannosaurus Rex? Personally I'm glad they are gone. The images of cute little Harp Seal babies being bludgeoned to death every year is horrifying, but have you ever squished a spider? What is the difference, because spiders aren't cute? We are part of the ecology, and we save baby seals because they are cute and don't care about spiders because they are icky, and you know what, that is the spider's problem!

Here is a scary thought. One expert I've read about suggests if the problem gets any worse, we should pave all roads in white concrete, and paint all roofs white to reflect heat away from Earth instead of absorbing it.

I don't know about you, but I'm damn glad I'm white! As much discrimination as African Americans (gave in to PC) have to deal with, now they will be blamed for Global Warming! "If we removed all black people, it would be the equivalent of taking 20,000 cars off the road."

While we are at it, there are just too damn many people on this planet. All that breathing in of oxygen and breathing out of carbon dioxide can't be good for the environment. I do my part; twice a day I hold my breath for 1 minute. Does Al Gore do that?

I've been on this Earth for 63 years, and you know what, the leaves are always off the trees the day after Thanksgiving, every year. And if the temperature is warming, won't those leaves stay a little bit longer? Won't they continue to change that horrible greenhouse gas back into oxygen a little longer? Have the computer models factored that into their equation? I'm guessing no.

Are the arctic ice caps shrinking? Probably, but are ice caps growing elsewhere? Not if it is an inconvenient fact. I've read that Admiral Bird's original camp in Antarctica is now covered by 100 feet of ice! What about those pictures of the glaciers sliding into the sea? Very scary. What the HELL did the Titanic run into? Is this a new phenomenon?

The Earth is always changing. To be constant would be a miracle, but we can only adapt. We are not so powerful that we can control the climate. Suppose we could control the climate. Talk about starting wars! Russia would be complaining, "Hey can we have a little heat up here!" The mid east would be screaming, "turn up the air for Mohammed's sake!" Who would make the decisions what temperature should be what? I say lets clean up the air, and find new energy sources, but leave the climate up to God.

Maybe it's just me.

NEWS FLASH – Six weeks after the above skeptical Global Warming rant was written comes allegations based on emails from Global Warming experts that all the raw data used to create the computer models have been destroyed. Further emails show these experts have been encouraged to hide the fact that temperatures have actually fallen in the last decade. This story has been on the internet for two weeks and has yet to be covered by ABC, CBS, or NBC. Liberals on Capitol Hill are very upset. "This is a crime", they assert, "and we're going to get to the bottom of it."

They are crying for a complete investigation as to whom and how these emails were obtained. They are worried about the computer hacking crime, and not the disturbing questions these emails raise. I seem to remember the guy who stole the Pentagon Papers which shined a bad light on the Viet Nam war and the Nixon administration being hailed as a hero.

Does this scare anyone else, or is it just me?

RT – Whatever happened to "however, but, and yet"? Why were they replaced by "having said that", and "that being said"? However, but and yet used to work just fine and take up so much less space.

Just a thought.

WHAT IF?

So many gifted and talented people today are lucky they were born at the right time and place for their special abilities to be used and appreciated. How many truly talented individuals lived an ordinary life because the world was not ready for their particular talents?

If Mickey Mantle was born in 1850, he would have grown up and died as just another coal miner. If Bill Gates was born in the mid-west 200 years ago, he would have been the worst farmer in Kansas! "That poor Billy Gates keeps mumbling about Windows, and a paperless society. What a wacko; that dumb geek can't even grow corn!"

What about the thousands of talented black slaves who labored in the fields, talents never to be discovered? I picture three slave masters at the local bar bitching about their jobs over a pint or two:

"Man I've got this kid can't pick cotton for shit. No matter how hard I whip him, Tiger won't pick it, he grabs a stick and hits the cotton balls into the basket! Impressive, but slow as Hell."

"You think that's bad, I got a slave so fast, I can't even hit him. Not only that, but he's so damn arrogant he recites poetry as he avoids the leather,

"Don't care how you swing that thing, this young man won't feel the sting. Gonna dodge and dip to get away, do not care what you say, can't nobody whip Cassius Clay".

The third laments, "I got a boy, Obama, I caught trying to organize the other slaves. As I led him away in shackles he just held them up and shouted "Chains we can't believe in!" Boy's so damn charming even white folks voted to let him go!"

Could have happened!

RT - What about those TV ads for security systems? The house is broken into, alarms go off, and you get a call from a guy who looks like Superman asking if anything is wrong. I'm thinking the real guy on the phone is a short, fat pervert who is pissed off that his need to call interrupted his online porn viewing.

RELIGION

I cannot tackle this subject without getting philosophical, and I hate philosophers. Really smart people wasting their time pondering questions like "If a tree falls in the forest and no one is there to hear it, does it make a sound?" That's an easy one, YESSSSS! I know some of you are asking, "But how do you really know?" Please, empirically I know that anything I've ever dropped makes a sound! If a pin dropped in the forest it would make a sound for Christmas sake! Stop thinking, and go invent something! The same people asking "how do you know"; believe without question that the Earth's temperature has risen 1 degree the last one hundred years, and they could not even tell if that degree was Fahrenheit or Celsius. Big difference, probably 50%. But I digress.

First of all, I believe in God. A wise old man with a long white beard, I don't know. To say Man was created in the image of God seems a bit egotistical to me. I believe in God as some life force far too complex for anyone to visualize. That's what makes him God. Some force somehow turned a bunch of chemicals, or molecules and over time developed them into the world as we know it. Kind of fantastic don't you think?

There are some scientists who believe they can explain formation of gasses and chemicals that interact in such a way over time to explode into suns, and planets, water and micro organisms which also over time developed into the world as we know it today.

Come on now! Where the heck did that first molecule come from? It then developed into animals and plants, which all interact to create the evolution of millions of species without any direction? HMMMMM.

I have heard the explanation philosophically described as "IF you had an infinite number of monkeys with an infinite number of typewriters over an infinite amount of time you would eventually get a great novel." Similarly given an infinite amount of time the world could be created. It is all just chance and evolution, no direction. I'm thinking even an infinite number of monkeys could never change the paper in a typewriter. If they used computers and Microsoft Word before that novel was created don't you think that damn monkey would forget to press save. At best, over an infinite amount of time you might get "To be or not to be, that is the br@&Gths".

Given the existence of this force, God, how to worship? I am a Christian. I choose Christianity as first I was born to a family of Christians, and second, let's face it, Christians have the best holidays! I do have one problem with Christianity, the part of Christ dying for our sins, and then rising from the dead. I have a hard time with that. I try to accept it for the sake of the really neat Holidays.

It is strange how people have trouble with the Holy Ghost concept, yet they buy into creepy ghost stories. There is no doubt that Christ was real, and was an amazing person who marched into town expecting to be crucified and still asked for forgiveness for his crucifiers. He was one tough Jew to be sure.

Jews refuse to accept Jesus as the Messiah, I think this is because given their reputation as shrewd business people, they will not accept that they made the worst trade in history. The son of God for a common thief! No money, no prophet to be named later, straight up Jesus for Barabbas!

It is difficult to worship an unknown force or entity, so worshiping the personification of God works for me.

The best Christian faith is Catholicism. Sin, screw up in anyway, and you simply confess it, a few Hail Mary's, and you are good to go. Protestants, especially WASPS do not so easily get relief from guilt, and hence tend to be a bit up tight. Black Protestants manage to somehow avoid this guilt. They sing, dance, swoon and have a grand old time. They rejoice in life. I think maybe they have it right. Being a WASP is not great.

I love the Jews. Here is a culture that has been pushed around forever, enslaved and then thrown out of Egypt, forced to wander around without a home, led into gas chambers by the Nazis, and yet saddled with a reputation of being pushy. Come on Jews, push back! If Hitler had been successful, look what we could have lost. A Jew gave us a cure for Polio, thank you, banking systems, thank you very much, days off at school, thank you again. These are a truly compassionate people who respect life and expect to give back.

You think health care is expensive, imagine it without Jewish doctors. The reason for so many Jewish lawyers is someone has to defend their families from malpractice suits.

I do have a slight problem with Muslims (no fatwa please). They are way too sensitive. Go on a warpath over cartoons of Mohammed with a bomb on his head? Have a sense of humor. You do blow shit up! And what is to say this cartoon is the **Prophet** Mohammed? Half of the population is named Mohammed. If showing a depiction of the Prophet Mohammed is verboten, how do you know the cartoon is of the Prophet? Who knows what he looks like?

Also this 40 virgin thing has me scratching my head. If I blow myself up, I don't want to meet 40 virgins in Heaven. Give me 3 horney sluts!

Maybe it's just me.

Of the major Religions, all believe (to my limited knowledge) in one God, and in some form of afterlife. Hindus believe in reincarnation, a nice concept if the first time around was good, not so nice if you spent 30 years cleaning up after sacred cows.

The way I see it, as long as you lead a good life, do no harm, respect others, and appreciate what you had; when you pass on, you have a shot at whatever it is we may call Heaven.

WASPS may get a lecture from God (pronounced GoDDD by protestant preachers). "I gave you a sense of humor, sex, alcohol, tobacco and other drugs (to be used in moderation) and you did not take full advantage of these things. Go sit in the corner for a few eons, and think about what you have done!" Eventually you can get in.

Jews; "You put up with enough crap, come on in; oh, and have some bacon".

Muslims, "I know you appreciate your creator, but bowing down five times a day every day? A simple thank you would have done. I get it; I'm God for Mohammed's sake. Well you just didn't know any better; so.... you're in too...... but please.... don't touch the virgins!"

THE REVERAND AND THE LAWNMOWER

I seldom went to church after high school. The exception was Easter Sunday. Mom loved the Easter Sunday Sunrise service. She would have us all up and dressed by 4:30 AM Easter Sunday, to catch the 5:00 AM Sunrise service. The most unusual service I can ever remember was Sunrise service in Easton Md. 1978.

It was a beautiful crisp Sunday morning, sunrise over an Eastern Shore creek, with a crab fisherman working his lines from a traditional Eastern Shore crab boat in the background. Insufficiently dressed for the cold as usual, the entire Hagy clan shivered and shifted from foot to foot as we waited for the service to start.

This traditional service combined three Easton, MD. Religious factions every year. Each year the sermon was given by a different denomination of Christianity. There was a Catholic Priest, an Episcopal Minister, and Baptist Reverend from the local Black church.

This year the sermon was delivered by the Episcopal Minister. The Priest offered a prayer, the Black Reverend read a scripture and the Episcopal Minister arose to give the Easter sermon. The priest sat on his left, the Baptist, ready to punctuate the sermon in the way common to the Black Baptist tradition part dance, part religious rap to his right; the Minister began his sermon.

"Friends, several years ago my lawn mower would not start"

"Wouldn't start"

"My wife informed me there was a repair shop 20 miles away in St, Michaels."

"Praise the Saint"

At this point Marybeth, seven at the time, yanked on my coat horrified that the Baptist was a nut and was being disrespectful of the service. She was not familiar with the Baptist point man tradition. I had to quietly assure her that "Praise God's" were quite all right.

"It was noon Saturday and the shop closed at one. If I wanted it fixed, I needed to leave right away."

"Tell it Rev"

"As I prepared to load the mower in my trunk, I was distracted by my daughter."

"Praise the children"

"I then got into the car and was off to the repair shop."

"Tell it"

"Half way to the shop, I realized that because of the distraction"

"Distracted"

"I might not have loaded the mower in the car."

"Tell it Rev"

"Now I could not stop and go back to see if I loaded the mower, because I would not have time before the shop closed"

"Tell it….rev?"

I knew by the Black Minister missing a beat, that he was thinking what we all were thinking, "Dude, stop the car and check the trunk". But the sermon went on.

"Should I go back and miss closing time, or continue on, having faith that the mower was in the trunk?"

"Faith, praise GOD"

Pull over and check the trunk, I thought with everyone else.

"I decided to continue on my way, with faith that the mower would be in the trunk."

"Praise God"

"When I arrived at the shop and checked the trunk my faith was rewarded."

"Praise God"

"The mower was in the trunk all along."

"Tell it, Tell it"

"And so friends it is this same faith that brings us here today on this blessed Sunday............"

On the way home, after service Chris commented, "Well I guess someone had to give the worst Easter sermon ever."

"Praise God"

Note: For anyone who does not believe this story, three years later our family stood in frozen sunrise astonishment as this same minister delivered the exact same sermon. This time the Baptist did not miss a beat. Not even I would make that up.

RT - Why do appliances like tooth brushes, electric razors and mixers have multiple speeds? Does anyone actually use low? Other than shifting thru speeds to simulate a race car, what idiot thinks, "gee, my teeth seem pretty clean, I'll just use low"? Or "I've got plenty of time to get to work, let's just shave on low today." I use a 60 year old Waring Blender with just one speed, puree, and it is just fine! OK, pulse comes in handy; it is called turning the switch on and off several times!

I guess it's just me.

SALES AND GUARANTEES

What is a sale? When you buy a $50 sweater for only $20, you really bought a $20 sweater that the store tried to rip someone off by selling it at $50! Stores do not give stuff away to be nice. "This beautiful dining room set ordinarily costs $3000, but if you act right now, I can sell it to you for $1500!" What, tomorrow you might suddenly come to your senses, and realize you're losing money at $1500? I think I'll come back in a week and see if you've gone completely loony and give it to me for nothing.

I once had a car salesman ask me "How much profit do you think I should make on this sale?" I said, "I don't care if you lose your shirt and get fired. What is the best price you can get for me?"

Sales people think we are all idiots, and we usually act in a way which reinforces that impression. After just 5 minutes, this guy is practically my best friend, and the next day when I try to return that shirt with one sleeve longer than the other he suddenly does not know me from Adam! "Did you buy that shirt here? Are you sure?" Yes I'm sure, don't you remember, the color goes with my eyes, and somehow makes my butt look extra firm…. Remember? I hate sales people!

Guarantees ooh, ah, what are they good for? Absolutely nothing. (To the tune of the classic "WAR")

I bought a Ginsu knife 40 years ago that snapped in two. Can someone tell me where to go to get back my $19.95? It was guaranteed for 50 years. Damn, where did I put that receipt? How much does it cost in shipping and handling to send it back? Cost $7.95 when I got it. Shipping and handling, there is a rip off, "BUY ONE FOR JUST $9.95 and get the second (worthless piece of crap) for FREE....just add an additional $7.95 in shipping and handling. When did it cost so much to mail a magic cork screw? I'm thinking these con artists give away a 50 cent piece of crap, and make $5 on shipping and handling!

Buy a brand new 50 inch screen high def TV, after listening to a 20 minute spiel on what a great product you are about to purchase, and the next question you get is "Do you want to buy a guarantee on that?" Jeeze, 20 minutes on how good this TV is, and you ask me to pay more in case it doesn't work? Here is my guarantee. I guarantee that if I get home and this thing doesn't work, I will be back here in 10 minutes screaming like a Banshee (is that insulting to Banshees?, and what is a Banshee?) until you give me one that does work!

I bought a new car 3 years ago, and the salesman raved about a 10 year or 100,000 thousand mile guarantee on the power train. What the Hell is a power train? Have you ever heard anyone say, "Car broke down the other day, blown power train."? I haven't. I'm thinking the power train is a made up term for something that sounds like a big deal but does not even exist! Kind of like a fornastat. Thanks for the guarantee. You've got a deal. I'd ask "What the heck is a power train?", but I am a guy, and there ARE rules!

TEENAGERS

Also easy, Teenagers are horrible, pimply-faced creatures who will do the opposite of whatever you ask because they are so smart and you are so stupid, you can't possibly understand how they feel about anything! Teenagers should be shipped away somewhere for 6-8 years, until you become smart and start to understand stuff again!

Parents, if you don't know, "What Ever" (pronounced WHAT' ever) is teenage code for "Fuck you"! Kind of like a grownup's "You have a great day now". "What Ever" should not be a tolerated response from a Teenager. You don't agree…"WHAT' ever".

One final word, pull your pants up, your undies are showing, and baseball hats should either be worn peak in the front to shade the sun, or peak in the back so the wind will not blow it off. The peak in any other position is only to make you look stupid, and it does.

Fortunately teenagers eventually grow to become real adults, and take care of you when you actually do become too stupid to take care of yourself.

It all comes back to bite you in the butt!

RT - If man is so smart, why did it take so long to invent the self sticking stamp?

BIRTHDAY PARTIES

When did birthday parties for kids become such a big deal? When I was a kid I could invite three or four friends for cake and ice cream, a game of pin the tail on the donkey, open up presents, say thank you very much, bye bye. No big deal. Now these parties have become competitive. Everyone is invited, can't hurt any feelings, and if Johnny had his party at Chuckey Cheese (four year olds aren't too scared of that giant f-ing rat) then somehow your kid's party has to be even better! These parties cost $500-$1000 every year, not to mention the costs of all those presents, plus gas and time to go to at least one party a week!

Could we please just agree to send a card, and dump all that money into a College Fund? And what genius invented the "Goody Bag"? If the little brats don't get an assortment of pencils and plastic crap-toys they are very upset! It's not their birthday why does everyone have to go home with something? They all have $200 IPods, $400 Play Station VI's, and God knows what else at home. Do they really need that plastic puzzle with a stupid bb to keep from being bored?

By the way, there are two words which make you want to wring a child's neck, "I'm bored". You're bored! Go make some sneakers like the six year olds in Indonesia; they're never "bored".

I'm sure it's just me.

RT - Sunrises and Sunsets are AWESOME, The Washington Monument is AWESOME, the Internet is AWESOME, the latest Hanna Montana CD, or new pair of shoes, is NOT AWESOME.........Dude. Now, having said that......never mind, it must just be me.

SPELLING

My sister-in-law complains that I am not a good speller. I could fiegn ignorance, but she is correct. The main reason for this deficeincy is I was just not an hier to the good spelling gene. My parents were very intelligent, but thier ability to spell correctly was just a foriegn concept. Wierd how that happens! This inability to spell does weigh heavily on me. Iether I am lazy or stupid. I hope that niether is true. Face it, spelling is just not an exact sceince. For the time bieng, I choose not to worry about my spelling; I will just enjoy my liesure and not have a siezure over this problem. Even Ienstien had a problem with spelling. If not for that old school rhyme, "I before E except after C" I would be totally helpless. If you follow this simple rule, there is no need for presceince or omnisceince. It doesn't matter if you are religious, or an athiest. If there is any question about spelling with "ie", or "ei", I find this rule to be sufficeint. (If in a Hotel you could always consult with the Conceirge.) So I will just sit back, enjoy a glass of Budwieser and forget it.

Sharpen up that red pencil Judy.

RT – After the first wash it is perfectly ok to mix colors with whites. I do it all the time and never have any problem!!

SPORTS

I love sports, but surprise; there is a list of things which drive me crazy!

GOLF – Who is the idiot who yells at every shot Tiger hits, "Get in the hole!"? He even yells it on the first shot on par five holes. Tiger is good, but please. Thankfully no one seems compelled to shout "you da man" after every drive anymore. I wonder if this was the same moron.

Greatest Golfer Ever – Sorry Jack, it is Tiger.

Bowling – Any time someone throws the ball between two pins on a split conversion attempt, does someone have to raise his arms signaling a successful field goal? This was very funny thirty years ago, but it is starting to get a little tired.

Why does the TV bowling expert try to insert psychology into a bowling match? "He wants to strike here, Bob, to put some pressure on his opponent". This game is very simple. You want to throw a strike every time, not to apply pressure on the opponent, but to throw a damn strike! That's like saying a wrestler "wants to pin his opponent here, Bob, to really put the pressure on his opponent".

One thing I like about bowling versus golf is I hardly ever lose a ball bowling.

Football – TV needs a color commentator, but every play? We saw what happened! Unless there was something unusual which requires an explanation or some special insight based on your special knowledge, please shut up? Don't worry about the women watching who may not fully understand the game. Just announce periodically where the game is being played. That seems to concern women; guess they want to know what the weather is like. An occasional comment on uniform color will also make them happy.

Every time a receiver touches the ball but does not make the catch the color guy has to say, "Al, he's just gotta make that catch." Have you ever played the game? It is just not that easy. And if he's gotta make that catch and he doesn't, is the game over?

Does this bother anyone else? Third and six and the receiver runs a five yard pattern and is tackled one yard short of the first down. "Al, doesn't he know where the yard marker is? He's gotta go to the yard marker". Does it not even occur to these idiots that the defense also knows where the first down is and defends it?

At least the guy with the rainbow afro and JOHN 3:16 sign is finally gone from every single game. How many non born-agains did he convert?

The D and the FENCE was very funny 25 years ago. Do we still have to see it at every game? We get it; very cute, very clever. Come up with something else! How about six noses with fingers up them (pick six) or a big sack and the letter M (sack'm), AH and a fence (offense), or a torn stocking - 2 day and a light bulb (run to daylight)? Anything! Come on. These are college students, come up with something clever.

Coaches: you get the team all revved up exhorting "go out and hit someone", "take no prisoners", "this is our house", and then get upset when one of your roid-rage players commits a personal foul....DUH.

Here is my favorite. "Go out and give me 110%". Wouldn't anything over 99.9% kill you?

Another coaching gem: "We're going to find out today who wants to win this game the most." As a 170 pound tackle lining up against a 240 pound guard with no neck, I was pretty sure the guy with no neck wanted it more than I did!

Could we please move Super Bowl Sunday to Saturday? This game starts at 8:30 PM, with commercials and a ridiculously long half time show; it ends around 12 midnight. Spencer watches football all season long, and then falls asleep before the championship game is over. At least declare the day after Super Bowl a national holiday; nobody gets anything done at work the next day anyway. Combine MLK day with President's Day.

I hate the Super Bowl party. This is usually an excuse for someone to show off their new giant flat screen TV. You can't even watch the damn game with the women gabbing, asking where the game is being played, commenting on the uniforms or asking stupid questions. Excuse me ladies, but when it is fourth and ten, "Are they kickin or stickin" is not an appropriate question. When the commercials come on, the men are shushed! The half time show is just for the women; put it on before the game.

I think it's just me.

Matt Snell

Story about football: His Senior year, Chris was the fastest high school football player on Long Island-for five yards. He was as fast as anyone for fifteen yards; beyond that he could not put it in fourth gear. His short legs kept churning, and defensive backs kept catching up. He was famous for quick openers where he was past the line and linebackers before they even knew what hit them, and then it was off to the races where his sheer will alone would get him to the end zone ahead of the faster defensive backs. Reaching the end zone after running seventy-five yards (150 in long legged yards) he would take off his helmet and throw up! Today this would be a penalty for excess celebration.

The big game that year for Chris' team was against Carle Place. I remember during an 8th grade game where I was playing against Carle Place, watching the Varsity run wind sprints. One Carle Place back continually finished 10–15 yards ahead of the pack in these sprints. Turns out it was Matt Snell, future star of the NY Jets Super Bowl III win.

Come the big game, Manhasset (Chris' team) and Carle Place were both undefeated. In the fourth quarter with Carl Place leading 14-12, (two Matt Snell runs and two Matt Snell PATS), Chris took off through the line and was past the linebackers heading for the end zone when out of nowhere came a Matt Snell elbow and Chris went down like a rock! Somehow in that game I served as water boy (first and only time). When Chris blinked open his eyes and saw me with a plastic squirty ketchup bottle of water, his only words were "What the Hell are you doing here?" Then he closed his eyes again. Game over.

Mom always hated Matt Snell for that elbow!

Baseball – There is a new thing today, where every time a batter hits a home run, he looks up to the sky and points in an "all praise is to God" kind of way…… Could we have a shot of the pitcher looking up with palms held outward in a "what the fuck did I do kind of way"? I'm thinking God does not take sides in sports.

This really yanks my crank; from the beginning of Baseball the short term for "Runs batted in" has been RBI's. Lately some sports writers have decided that since it is **RUNS** batted in the short form should be RBI, or even worse- R'sBI. **Just stop it!** It is RBI's! "Al he has 3 RBI this game" just does not sound right!

Almost as bad is the attempt to refer to the foul line and the foul pole as the fair line or pole. Yes, if it hits the foul line or pole it is fair, but if it is on the foul side of the line or pole it is foul. The line and the pole mark the beginning of foul territory. Baseball is all about tradition, stop trying to change the terminology. The object of the game is to score by reaching home plate, should we change the name of the game to Plateball?

Greatest Baseball Player Ever - Babe Ruth was the most influential in terms of creating baseball's booming popularity. He invented the home run. Before The Babe, most hitters slapped the ball to the open field. However, the greatest player ever was Willie Mays. Willie did it all. He was a great fielder who could run down anything and make a basket catch (cool), hit with power, hit for average, and created havoc running the bases. This is from a lifelong Yankee fan.

Basketball – Why does it take fifteen minutes to play the last thirty seconds? And why does the last thirty seconds always come just as dinner is served? When a white point guard makes a nice pass, he is "a real student of the game". When a black point guard makes the same nice pass, "he just instinctively knows where to go with the ball". I think this is more racist than Howard Cosell's famous "Look at that little monkey run" comment. As bad as that commentary was, I doubt Cosell meant it to be racist. I think it was just an instinctive call!

Greatest Basketball Player Ever – Bill Russell did not have the stats: scoring, assists, rebounds, steals, or blocked shots. Someone was always better in terms of stats. What Bill Russell did was win! He always won. In college he led the University of San Francisco to two NCAA championships and 55 straight wins. As a pro his Celtics won 11 of 13 NBA championships and as a coach he won two NBA championships. Stats are great, but no athlete knew how to win like Bill Russell.

Greatest Tennis Player, Bowler, or Hockey Player– Don't care!

Greatest Swimmer - Michael Phelps. (Also don't care, but had to get one white guy in here.)

Figure Skating – FIGURE SKATING!!!

Olympic Athletes – To be sure Michael Phelps's many gold medal wins was a great accomplishment. He also has turned it into a multi-million dollar payoff. Al Oerter won the discus throw four Olympics in a row. He never made a dime off this feat. And he practiced every day after work for twenty years. That is a real Olympian!

Greatest Olympian-Al Oerter

Lacrosse – This is a great game which will never be commercially popular as it is impossible to watch on TV.

German Measles And Comic Books

Jim was a very good lacrosse player. He made the Long Island High School All Star team which in those days would make him one of the best players in the country. I played in Junior High and thus was never able to see Jim play.

I did have a chance to finally see Jim in a game, the annual HS all star game. I was very excited the night before this game but I woke up the next morning with a high fever and spots all over my body. German measles! I was bummed out all day, holed up in my dark bed room, missing my only chance to see my big brother in action.

Late in the afternoon, I was awakened by Jim, his girlfriend, and a stack of comic books which they had brought. Jim did not say much, just threw the books (too which I was addicted) at me and said, "sorry you missed the game." To those who don't speak WASP, this means, "Wish you had been at the game. I love you Bro"… It made the Measles worth having.

Hunting and Fishing – I love fishing, but animal rights nuts want to ruin this activity. They claim cruelty to the fish, even though I let most of them go free. I guess the hook might cause some pain, but as some noted ichthyologist once said, "In the history of the world, no fish has ever died peacefully in its sleep. They grow old, slow, or sick, and another fish EATS THEM ALIVE!!" Does someone have to try and make me feel guilty about everything?

Now, hunting is different, and not something I would enjoy. It is very difficult to hunt and practice "shoot and release". I don't object to hunters, however, as there is something deep in our DNA which just wants to kill stuff! Better that Elmer Fudd bags a deer than I bag it with the front end of my Jeep.

If you watch fishing shows on TV, you know that every catch is "a nice fiiiish". Just to make it clear this is repeated several times. "That's a nice fiiish, nice fiiish"! A big fish apparently has shoulders. "Look at the shoulders on that one". I never see the shoulders. Also a popular comment is "check out the chunk on this one. Put together, "That's a nice fiiish, and he got some shoulders! Just check out the chunk, yes sir, that's a nice fiiish, nice fiiish"……Time for a commercial.

Hunters have to whisper, *"here comes a big buck, eight pointer, quiet, shhhh, easy, in my sights, come on baby turn, turn, hold it"……POW!! "That's a nice deeear, nice deeear, big buck, what a rack!!!"* After gutting the animal and lugging it back to strap onto the car, the hunter quenches his thirst and appetite at the local Hooters. *"Here comes a nice one, quiet, shhh, easy, in my sights, come on baby turn, turn."* WOW!! *"That's a nice baaabe, nice baaabe, big butt, what a rack!!!"* Hunters got class!

One big difference between hunting and fishing is it is safer to drink and fish. I'm not recommending anyone drink and do either, but come on, it happens. It is much easier to remove a hook from a cheek than it is to remove a bullet (usually a different cheek). Mistakes are easy to remedy in fishing, "darn, that fish is not in season, better throw it back". Not so easy in hunting. "Dang Jeb, that's a cow!" OOPS!

POOL-This is a game that for some reason everyone thinks he can play. Add that and the fact it is often played over a few beers and pool is the classic hustler's game.

I once sat out lunch at my college fraternity and a salesman came in waiting for lunch to end to peddle his mugs, hats and other fraternity crap. He asked if he could shoot some pool while he waited. I watched him throw out a rack and pocket every ball in machinegun like fashion.

When lunch ended he challenged one of the brothers to a game, and lost by one ball. He played another and lost again by one ball. Then, just to make it interesting the salesman casually asked," how about a buck a game." I said nothing, not being particularly fond of this "brother" (OK, I lied I don't like EVERYONE I've met). This salesman proceeded to take the "brother" five games in a row, everyone on the last shot, a lucky double bank shot, and won $10, a considerable sum for a college student in the sixties. The brother never knew what hit him, and I never told him!

RT - Why do Black athletes jump higher and run faster than Whites? That's right, I said it. Is that politically incorrect? Take a nationwide vote on that question; care to guess how it would come out? I believe the reason is genetic. Jimmy "The Greek" got fired for saying that. I'm already retired. I once read where some tribes in Africa used to hold a ritual where the young men would get in a circle and jump. The highest jumper would get his pick of a mate. Think that might lead to genetically superior runners and jumpers after thousands of years? Europeans with the best farms got their pick of mates. Do you know of any Black farmers?

Don't get angry, I'm just saying.

BOXING - This sport seems to be dying in popularity, partly because of the Ultimate Fighting craze. I still prefer boxing, but currently the sport lacks charismatic fighters. THERE IS ONLY ONE Mohammad Ali. He came along in the sixties and revived the sport. Boxing needs another Mohammad Ali.

Who would have won a fight between Mohammad Ali and Mike Tyson in their prime? Mohammad Ali. Ali always found a way to win, the Bill Russell of boxing. Tyson was a bully with tremendous speed and power, but Ali could also take a punch like no other, and had no quit in him. Ali would have frustrated Tyson with his speed, and when he got hit would not go down. Tyson would get careless trying to put him away, and Ali would hurt him. Once hurt, Tyson would quit. He was not used to being hurt.

WRESTLING - There are two wrestling sports, real and professional. Real wrestling is a true Spartan sport, demanding dedication, courage, and skill. It is not much fun to watch. Professional wrestling requires hard work, skill, painkillers and steroids. It is lots of fun to watch.

TENNIS - I Hate Tennis

SAILING - Is this a sport? Racing is, and since I used to race I will list it here as a sport. My Uncle Tom raced ocean sailboats, a sport, a passion, and a money eater. His description of Ocean Racing was to set up a lawn chair with a hose shooting spray at you, and place a meat grinder next to the chair. Every ten minutes put a hundred dollar bill in the meat grinder and turn the crank. That would be close to Ocean racing.

Boat Building

My brothers and I raced eleven foot boats which were restricted in design only by the eleven foot length and sail size. This unlimited restriction in design virtually guaranteed that Dad would design the best boat in the class. That was just Dad. He spent an entire winter designing and building a boat out of fiberglass which would not only be the fastest, but would also be swamp proof, a big problem for small boats raced by young inexperienced sailors. The sailors at our Ocean City Club were waiting the next spring for the much ballyhooed Hagy boat which was to be not just fast, but swamp proof as well.

Finally the boat was ready, with some delay because it would not fit up the basement stairs. Dad waited for Mom to go shopping. He then immediately got his trusty rip saw out and made a large hole through her hardwood oak floor in the den. He got the boat out, constructed a trap door to cover the hole and covered the trap door with a rug before mom got home. She wasn't mad when he told her—but it might have been the next year before he got around to it. (That's right current owner of 21 Borglum Rd., Manhasset, Long Island. That is why there is a big trap door under the rug in your den.)

Dad took his boat and tested it on Long Island Sound, Tragically because of an extra heavy deck, the boat was top heavy, and not sailable. It would turn over with virtually any shifting of weight. At least with the baffle sides (the first of its type in a small boat to my knowledge) the boat was unsinkable.

It was a long summer, with many a joke about the Hagy boat.

Well, Dad did it again the next winter, redesigning and rebuilding a boat which for the next three summers was the fastest in the class, and totally unsinkable. It was total redemption for the old man. I told you he was smart.

Ultimately a boat, though very sinkable and unstable, was designed which was faster than Dad's. Dad was out of the boat building business, so Jim stepped in and using Dad's original design with a lighter deck, Jim and I rebuilt the original in the basement in only three weeks. A quick explanation of the process is needed here. First, using Dad's original design (minus the heavy deck) you build a plaster mold. Then using this you build another mold out of fiberglass, giving you a smooth inside which will then produce a fiberglass hull with a smooth outside.

Unfortunately, the good hull did not come out of the mold cleanly due to our haste to complete it in order to enter the upcoming final race series of the summer. Not one to quit, Jim tried to sand down the outside of the MOLD, refit it, and entered it in the series.

He finished third sailing a MOLD! This was with the completely rough surface which slowed the boat due to increased water resistance. That boat (mold) was then retired, never to sail again, but we felt that Dad's original design was somewhat redeemed. Jim was maybe nineteen when we did this. Jim was very smart!

Wide World Of Sports

Whatever happened to "Wide World Of Sports"? This was the only show which made the vast sports waste land between The Super Bowl and March

Madness bearable. Jim McKay could make even curling interesting. I want to see that poor bastard (not Jim McKay) slip off the ski jump one more time!

I think the demise of this show was the episode on White Dove Hunting. Jim McKay, some ex-football player and a couple of red necks discussed the thrill of White Dove Hunting in hushed reverent tones for about a half hour when suddenly you hear the cry, "Here they come".

The sky went dark from the white doves eclipsing the sun. McKay, the football player and the red necks were whooping it up and firing shotguns from their hip. White doves were falling in droves; still they kept coming and the "Sportsmen" kept firing. Dogs were running in circles, they didn't know whether to fetch, or what to fetch, while trying to dodge the falling birds!

I think some people found this episode offensive.

The Greatest Athlete Ever - Jim Thorpe, Bo Jackson, Bill Russell? Hands down it was Jim Brown! He was the greatest NFL running back ever. He was six foot two, 230 pounds and he ran a 9.2 hundred. He could have played virtually any position on the NFL field (in his time), including place kicker which he did in college (quick, name a Black place kicker). Jim Brown was an All-American in college at football, basketball (he once scored fifty points in a game) and lacrosse where it is said even today that he was the greatest lacrosse player to ever play the game! Do you think there will ever be a three sport Division 1 All-American player in college again? He did all this at a time when ¾ of the country wanted him to fail because he was Black! He then went on to become a successful actor, and the first Black man to have a romantic scene on screen with a White woman. Jim Brown did not take shit from anyone!

He is, however, contributing to Global Warming.

Greatest Sporting Event Ever - Although I am not a Hockey fan, the greatest game in any sport I have ever seen was the 1980 Olympic Hockey game USA vs. USSR. The game was televised on tape delay; I do not remember why. It was probably because nobody expected it to be competitive. The US had lost to the USSR in a pre-Olympic game by an 11-1 score. (Something like that anyway) The USSR was the overwhelming favorite to win the gold while the USA was hoping against hope for any medal at all. I recall between periods while the US was hanging in the game, which in itself was almost beyond belief, they showed a shot of celebration in the streets of Lake Placid. "Oh my God", I thought, "Did we tie"? I knew something good happened, but win never entered my mind as the Russian team was so dominant. When they won, on tape delay, it was just unbelievable. So much was the win unexpected, as the clocked ticked down the final seconds, Al Michaels made the famous call "Do you believe in miracles?, YES!"

Miracles do happen!

Many people forget that that game was not for the gold medal. To win the medal the US had to beat Yugoslavia (I think) the next morning, a game they also were not favored to win. Win they did and many a non hockey fan set their alarms to watch that early morning game.

THREE GOLF STORIES

During High School and College, my best friend was Charlie Widmer. Charlie was what I will later describe as a border line Misfit in school, I was a Tweener. Charlie was not a big guy, maybe 5' 7" 160 pounds, but he had powerful forearms and wrists from playing baseball. Charlie was a tough kid as he was often used as a punching bag by his older brother. He also tended to get in trouble from time to time. His father passed away when he was eight and he was unsupervised after school as his Mom had to work. Charlie's mom, whom he called Jessie and I called Aunt Jess encouraged the relationship between Charlie and me as she felt I might keep him out of trouble.

In the summer, we worked for Charlie's cousin whom we called "Mr. Big", installing underground sprinkler systems. On weekends we played golf. We played at the local county course, Ashbrook, whose rock hard fairways allowed for prodigious drives of up to 300 yards. I played to about a 12 handicap, and Charlie, despite his weird Billy Madison like baseball stance, scored about the same.

THE WORST SHOT EVER

One day on the seventh hole at Ashbrook, a one hundred and ten yard par three and the easiest hole on the course, Charlie set up to fire at the hole with a nine iron. As he swung he must have lifted his head because he barely managed to strike the ball with the end of the club head. The ball went off at a ninety degree angle on a low trajectory. It struck the ball cleaner and returned straight back to Charlie. Charlie's baseball instincts kicked in and he swung again lifting a foul pop directly behind him into the woods and hopelessly lost.

"Let's see" I calculated, "Two swings, two strokes for hitting a ball still in motion, and a two stroke penalty for a lost ball. I'd say you are lying six, hitting seven." "Six hell" Charlie replied, "If ever a shot deserved a Mulligan, that was it!"

Mulligan granted.

"FORE……Mother FUCKers"

Late one August Sunday, Charlie and I had just finished playing eighteen holes. Ashbrook was amazingly not crowded at the time. There was no wait on the ninth tee, so we decided to squeeze in another nine holes.

By the eleventh hole we caught up to a very slow foursome and had to wait on every shot. The foursome behind us also caught up and made little attempt to hide their impatience. This group was four guys several years older than we were, and probably were in a rush to get home before their wives got upset at their late finish.

The foursome behind was complaining about the slow play loudly enough for us to hear, and in a manner belligerent enough to entice us to let them play thru. As the delay was not our doing, we were in no mood to accede to their obvious wish.

After driving on the par five twelfth hole, Charlie and I waited for the green to clear before hitting our second shots. Even though it was doubtful we could reach in two, courtesy demanded we wait. Our instinct, that the foursome behind wanted us to allow them to play thru was confirmed when we heard a loud "FORE". Their longest hitter drove without waiting for us to hit. The ball landed fifteen yards behind us and rolled right beside Charlie.

In the world of guys and fights this was clearly a push. A non-fighter like myself would just wave them through and be done with it. Charlie did not look to start a fight as were those behind us, but he was also not afraid to get his ass kicked. He had been in fights and won; he had been in fights and had his ass kicked. In the world of guys and fighting, it is not the guy who starts the fight you need to fear, but the guy who despite the odds is not afraid to be whooped.

Charlie decided to push back. He adjusted his stance to face our tormentors, and with the best three wood of his life (Charlie was always good under pressure) launched a shot directly back at the aggressors. The ball landed in the middle of the foursome and bounced off the tee into the woods. It was then that Charlie hollered out the not so traditional golf warning, "FORE....**Mother FUCKers**."

"Shit", I thought, "I'm about to get an ass kicking." Apparently the bullies thought twice before starting up with a guy, or two guys for all they knew, who were not afraid of taking a beating; particularly not when two-irons were potentially involved. We did not see or hear from these SOBs the rest of the round; in fact I think they just packed up and left. Charlie never even noticed.

"Six iron aughta bout doit."

One Saturday Charlie and I decided to play at the less crowded public course, Oak Ridge. Oak Ridge was not a county course and cost $6.00 to play as opposed to the $1.75 fee at Ashbrook. Flush from cashing our $65 paychecks we did not care.

We were about to tee off as a twosome when the local Pro's assistant asked to join. Not a problem, and so we teed off with Jimmy, a sixteen year old hot shot who advised us he was planning to skip college and go for his PGA card. Jimmy was good, to be sure. He out drove us every hole by a good 40 to 50 yards. His iron shots were crisp and true and he knew the course. He would land his shots just short of the green and allow the ball to roll to the pin. The greens were just too hard to fire at the pin.

As the round progressed we could tell by Jimmy's increased confidence and swagger, that as good as he was, he was having the round of his life. By the fourth hole, Jimmy was one under par. After six he was two under, and on the eighth hole he sank a 30 footer to go to three under par. As we teed off the ninth, Jimmy's every action showed even more swagger in an attempt to act as if this round was nothing unusual for him.

The ninth hole was 425 yards uphill and into the wind. Charlie and I both hit decent drives followed by three woods just short of the green. Jimmy approached his drive, sixty yards past ours, flipped a club out of his bag, caught it in midair by the grip and said to no one in particular but loud enough for us to hear, "six iron aughta bout doit."

He launched another crisp shot toward the green, only this one was slightly off to the left. It landed with a splash in the trap protecting the left of the green.

Charlie and I both chipped to within ten feet of the flag, and Jimmy grabbed his wedge. Still cocky he remarked "gonna have to put some touch on this one."

Charlie and I said nothing.

Jimmy put a little too much touch on his shot. It just missed clearing the lip and rolled back to his feet. Jimmy now said nothing. Charlie and I remained silent as well. Jimmy's next shot was too flush; the ball sailed over the green and rolled into another trap. Jimmy said nothing as he crossed the green with noticeably less swagger.

Charlie and I said nothing.

Jimmy flailed at the ball and a ton of beach hit the green. We saw no ball and said nothing. Jimmy swung again and the ball sailed over the green, over the trap and into the very deep rough. The ball was followed by his wedge, a very nice side armed end over end toss which we admired silently. Jimmy crossed the green, picked up his bag and flung it about ten yards. Pulled that toss we noted. With his clubs randomly strewn throughout the rough, Jimmy stomped off to the pro shop without saying a word.

Charlie and I said nothing.

Charlie then lined up his putt and before making his stroke was barely able to blurt out through his laughter, "six iron aughta bout doit!"

Needless to say, we both three putted.

I'm pretty sure Jimmy never got his PGA tour card.

LOTTERIES

For years, gambling in any form was illegal in every state except Nevada. Gambling was a sin, it preyed on the poor, led to poverty, criminal behavior, and Heroin addiction (proceeded, of course, by talking back to parents). Then, when States needed a new revenue source to pay for their overspending, preying on the poor suddenly became OK. They are doing it anyway, the politicians would assert, and the profits go to the mob. Well, the mob never advertised on TV and every newspaper to garner more clients. I'll buy a two dollar scratch–off every now and then, but I cringe when I see people of obvious meager means pull fifty bucks from their pay envelope and throw it away to the State.

The States all said every dollar will go to schools. HMMMM, then why do my property taxes go up every year? I love how these suckers throw away their hard earned money, (or welfare checks). When I do purchase a ticket, I quietly say, "I'll take a quick pick please." The poor lottery addicted fools are proud of their lottery expertise. They announce with great pride and loud voice, "Let me have a 10 spot on 27, 15, 44, 8 and 12, and reverse it, put it in the bucket, box it, flip flop it and divide by 2!" Fifty dollars later they will advise how they won twenty five dollars last month (which no doubt they tried to parlay, and it went right back to the State).

We now have legalized gambling of every form in virtually every State. Notice how low your taxes are? Perhaps States don't run stuff very well. In New York, their off track betting operation is in the red. Do they sell more lottery tickets to cover the loss? The Mob never lost any money. Of course the Mob doesn't have to deal with unions (except the ones they control). Well, they sort of have a union, but members are not allowed to strike. Or leave!!

When some slob does win a big lottery of millions of dollars, they invariably have their lives ruined. Divorce, over spending, behind on taxes, the winners generally still lose. Apparently living with multiple millions of dollars requires some knowledge of investing, self control, and the ability to say no to those new found friends and relatives.

It's just my opinion.

RT - Ladies, stop the Woo Hoo! I hate the Woo Hoo.

RACISM AND PREJIDICE

If I offend anyone in this section, (Why haven't you already been offended? Are you reading this?) Keep in mind my introduction. I like everyone I've met, and hate everyone else. I have only known three Muslims, so if I am hard on you guys more of you need to introduce yourselves to me. You also need a little better PR. Dropping two buildings which I watched being constructed, watched a human fly climb, a French crazy tightrope walker cross, a parachute jumper jump, and then watched these buildings come tumbling down with several close friends inside, swayed my opinions to the negative side. Suicide belts on teenagers and beheadings have also not helped your image. Sorry.

Racism is just wrong. I judge a person as MLK said, by the content of his character. I don't care if you are red, white, yellow, black, brown, green or blue.........OK, green and blue people do freak me out a little. Otherwise people are people.

Not that all people are alike. People from different origins have different characteristics. Asians have narrow eyes, Irish may have red hair, Africans are dark complexioned. Human nature is such that people tend to prefer those who look like they do. This is particularly a problem in the US where our population is so diverse. Some differences are genetic; some are cultural.

I do not want to be politically incorrect, so let me first state, Black people do not run faster or jump higher than white people. The one White dude in the Olympics just happens to get a really bad start every four years. The Irish don't drink, Asians aren't always good at math, Jews don't all know how to run a business, some Italians do take shit from somebody, WASPS aren't all uptight, some Muslims wear real belts, and Germans are not all war like and sometimes will cross the street against the light. Some Indians are bodybuilders, some Polish are lazy, and Mexicans don't always travel in threes (well as a personal observation they do, but I could be wrong).

The beauty of our country is in its diversity of people and cultures. Our population is made up of people who took great risks and overcame difficulties to come to this land to escape injustices or improve their life. We get the best of the best. Lazy, stupid, or un-ambitious people would not attempt to endure the difficulties and hardships of immigrating to a strange new land. Many Africans, of course, did not come of their own free will, but I suspect the consequences of horrible conditions on slave ships and harsh treatment under forced servitude meant the weak did not survive.

RT - Immigration is what makes this country great, but I wish some of our "guests" would not get angry at me because I cannot understand them. The other day I went to a gas station and this guy in a turban asks me "Gatch o chatch?"

"Excuse me."

"Gatch o chatch, GATCH O CHATCH!"

"What?"

"GATCH O CHATCH!!"

I did not have a clue; but not wanting to aggravate him any further I replied, "gatch". When it was time to pay I handed him a credit card and he went ballistic.

"That no gatch. That CHATCH!!"

WHAT IF – What if the south had been allowed to secede from the union? Would slavery (our country's greatest blemish) still exist today? Probably slavery would have lasted ten or fifteen more years, but would blacks have had to endure the same discrimination and implicit "slavery" that lasted another one hundred plus years? Did a million innocent people have to die? Would we have had the lingering hatred between the north and the south? Do you think the union wouldn't have eventually rejoined?

It's just a thought.

Back to racism. This is still a lingering problem, but the progress in my lifetime has been enormous. As a boy growing up in southern California the only

Black or Mexican people I ever saw were household help, or on posters in the post office. The only Asians I ever saw were Japanese gardeners. Indians were on "Rama of the Jungle", or the enemies of cowboys. Arabs were in Bugs Bunny cartoons, "Hassan Chop!" Nice images, huh. A Fag is what we called other kids if we wanted to taunt them (never even knew what a homosexual was until College, and still didn't really believe it!). A "Dirty Jew" is what we called people we really didn't like without even knowing what a Jew was. Imagine my shock when I moved to Long Island at age eight and found several of my new friends were Jewish? When we played eenie meenie minie mo, we did not catch a "tiger" by the toe, and I swear they sold liquorish candy tots called "nigger babies".

My Mom and Dad were truly good people, but grew up in an age even less enlightened than mine. I once was picked on by Peter Boyle. Mom's response was, "just stay away. The Irish are bullies and love to fight."

One day I came home from school complaining that this kid who I thought was my friend pegged me with a baseball for "No reason at all"! "What is his name", Mom inquired? "Carl Longerio." "Oh don't be upset" she replied. "The Italians are all crazy. He didn't mean a thing".

I can even remember in the late fifties watching a teenage lifeguard in Ocean City, N.J. whistling a grown Black man off the segregated beach and I did not blink an eye.

And so prejudice is imprinted on us all in our impressionable youth. I hope that with age and interaction with peoples of all types that I have overcome this early imprinting. (Muslims you gotta help me out on this).

Today we have a Black President, the second most powerful person in the world after Oprah, and people of all genders, sexual preferences, races and religions holding powerful positions in government and industry.

I recently watched a movie with Spencer, "Remember the Titans", a great movie about the integration of a Virginia High School football team in the early seventies. I had to pause the film many times to explain to Spencer why these players had so much trouble getting along. I was unable to get the concept of racial hatred through his mind. I finally just explained these groups each came from other sides of town and were former rivals. He seemed fine with that. I accepted his bewilderment as a good thing. He has plenty of time to get a history lesson.

I am not so naive as to believe prejudice and racism is no longer an issue in this country, but progress has been great.

Let me say that all problems between groups are not just the fault of the majorities. Years ago I had a young black co-worker, Russell, a great guy, funny guy, son of two school teachers, attended University of Penn, and at six foot three was one heck of a basketball player. Russell once related to me how he and his friends used to gather around little Jewish ladies on the subway, and glare. "You should see how scared they get just because we're black." I said, "Jesus, Russ, you're six three and glaring at them. I think that might be enough to scare anyone!" Russell, by the way, was tragically killed in a motorcycle accident at a young age leaving a widow and baby girl behind.

Russell was a really good chess player. We would play at lunch, and he usually kicked my butt. I don't think he was that much better than I was, but he played with attitude. When I would make a move, I'd leave my finger on the piece, scanning for any possible area of attack before finally making a move. Russell would scan the board, think for a minute, and then slam his piece to the new square, lean back and start talking smack as if this move put me in jeopardy. Even his bad moves got me flustered and generally caused my demise. Russell had attitude!

My work introduced me to a variety of people with whom I had never really had much contact. And true to form I liked everyone I met and with whom I worked.

I found the best way for me to break the ice was to attack stereotypes. My first year I worked alongside two militant black ladies, (this was when the Panthers were big). They hated me because I was white. I would intentionally get their names wrong and claim it was because they looked alike. I would go on a break and ask if they wanted me to bring back watermelon. I would tell them Al Jolson was my favorite artist. And I would beg them to go easy on me when you 'all take over. After a while they would just say, "Joe Hagy you're crazy", and they would poke fun at my WASP ness. (WARNING, improper use of this repertoire MAY RESULT IN DEATH.) At any rate we all learned a lot about each other and ended up good friends. They promised to protect me when the revolution came.

I made fun of the Puerto Ricans speaking Spanglish in the elevators, claiming I knew what they were saying. I blamed them for stealing my hubcaps, and threatened to take away their knives. We all had fun with how ridiculous these stereotypes were. If any conversation turned to sex I would stammer, "Hello, WASP here."

Going to breakfast with my orthodox Jew boss, I would taunt him with how good bacon was, and what he was missing. He once admitted to me that he ate Mahi Mahi, and when he found out that it was dolphin he hoped God would forgive him for eating a fish without scales. He was very relieved when

I explained that Mahi Mahi was dolphin, but not Flipper. I had fun with differences and stereotypes, and made many good friends.

The Irish are the only group I know that you can't make fun of. They will tell the jokes on themselves before anyone else can. Patty the drunk jokes, Mary the prude jokes, boiled food jokes, Irish Priest jokes. If you've heard any of them you probably heard them from an Irishman.

This is why I am so against political correctness. We all need to be sensitive. All situations are not alike, but when you tap dance around stereotypes and differences, the nine hundred pound gorilla never leaves the room. I have heard people trying to describe someone as, "Tall, quiet, thin, good looking and with short hair." The dude is BLACK for crying out loud. Did you not notice!

SEXUALITY

Touchy subject for a WASP, but here goes. I am obviously not an expert in this field. I lived through the entire sexual revolution, and never fired a shot. And I was married! Yes, I had three kids, I think I tossed and turned in my sleep a lot.

Sex was not discussed very much in my house, if at all. Discussions of the birds and the bees were about birds and bees. Lucy and Desi slept in separate beds. Sex in the films was a fade out, followed by the couple smoking cigarettes. I never understood why there was so much intrigue and drama over smoking a cigarette.

In eighth grade, we did have make out parties, and I learned the thrill of outside boobage. I never wanted a cigarette though. That was about it for me, until the revolution came. TV couples slept together, x-rated movies showed all, and I was married. I did take up smoking!

With limited knowledge and experience I do have opinions on the subject. First, I ultimately did learn that sex is good. It can be very good. Sometimes, however, it is just better to smoke.

Men will do or say almost anything for sex. I have even become a Liberal for sex. Sex is Man's most powerful drive, and is responsible for lies, thefts, murders, and most wars. What drove OJ Simpson to murder? Sex. What drives Bill Gates' success? Sex. What is the real cause of Muslim fanaticisms? Sex.

This is why I own stock in tobacco companies.

Women know sex is Man's greatest weakness, and often use (or don't use) sex as a weapon. They use or hold out on this precious commodity to get what they want. And so Man invented alcohol.

Sex takes many forms, and all are perverted to somebody. Thus it is seldom talked about in mixed company. There is the story of two convicts. One asks the other, "What are you in for?" The other responds," Bestiality."

"Bestiality, what is that?"

"Bestiality, that's having sex with animals, cows, goats, chickens…"

The first convict mulls this over and then responds, "Chickens, Yeeech!"

I happen to be a raging heterosexual. I have a hard time understanding members of the other team. In fact as stated earlier I did not know the other team even existed until my twenties. Members of the away team were referred to as eccentric, confirmed bachelors, spinsters, or Priests.

I have nothing against the other team. Without homosexuals where would we get hair dressers, designers, or FBI directors? I don't understand why women are attracted to men, never mind men attracted to men. Lesbianism, however, as previously stated, does make perfect sense to me.

Some say this inclination is by choice. I doubt it. With all the prejudice and social stigma attached to this behavior, who would make a conscious decision to be gay? It must have been horrible to have been gay in the dark ages. Never mind living in the closet, but not even knowing there were others with the same desires! I believe homosexuality must be genetic. It should be easy to prove. Hasn't some expert ever done a study on separated identical twins?

I have known and been friends with many homosexuals, and except for that sex thing, found them to be basically the same as anyone else. Once again, mutually making fun of the stereotypes breaks the ice. I was only offended one time, when someone referred to me as a "breeder". I can understand how hurtful it must be to be called a faggot, queer, sissy, or baloney smuggler. Couldn't he see how offensive it is to be seen as simply a "breeder"?

Here is an opinion that would get me locked up today. "NO, DAMMIT, GET YOUR HANDS OFF ME", means no. "Nooo, I don't think we should do this", means keep sweet talking, and hurry up before I change my mind! The reason teenage boys don't use a condom is the fear that any small delay is just enough to close the window of opportunity.

Have you seen the late night commercial endorsing a tube like contraption with a pump as the answer to sexual dysfunction in older men? They claim it is better than a pill, as it allows for spontaneity. HMMMM, "Gee honey, you're in the mood? Let me get out the enhancer and pump up. I'll just be a minute". Now there is a real turn on.

Then there is an ad which claims you can improve performance and SIZE with a non FDA approved pill. If the FDA doesn't have to approve this pill, it can only be a combination of vitamins and herbs. Probably it is just a sugar pill, which seems to be effective in curing 10% of everything anyway. Yet, this pill is sold by the millions!

How does anyone think this thing can increase size, and if it could, how does it know where to increase size? I'm thinking some men might be a little disappointed when they end up with one big toe larger than the other or really big ears, which is the only part of the human body which never seems to stop growing anyway. Does size really matter? This is hard to know as women will lie about this subject. I'm thinking if you've got a peanut, size matters, or if you're sporting a Louisville slugger you may be severely limited in sexual opportunity.

Well, I guess that is about all I have on this subject (was that a sigh of relief I just heard from my editor, Judy?). My WASPishness prevents further discussion. I am not a prude; suffice it to say my interests in this subject lie somewhere between women and chickens!

RT - I really hate the bastard that spiked Tylenol years ago. Because of him it is a pain in the ass to open just about anything.

INFLATION

When I was a kid, a hamburger cost twenty cents, five cents extra for a cheeseburger. A hotdog was fifteen cents, and virtually any candy was a nickel. My friend and I would gather soda bottles on the way to the local strip mall (there was a lot of construction along the way) and cash them in for enough money to bowl two games, eighty five cents with shoe rental, and have enough left for candy and a comic book.

Those were the good old days. Except, a twenty one inch color TV cost seven hundred and fifty dollars, and it only got seven channels. I Pods were real expensive, CDs hard to find, home movies were eight millimeter shown on a screen which took forever to set up, and pictures took a week to develop. Computers took up a building, the internet was not even anticipated by Jules Verne, and Dick Tracy's two way wrist radio was a pipe dream. Air conditioning was in movie theaters, not homes or cars. Clocks were analog and worked in new cars for about two weeks. Radios weighed about twenty pounds, and on a good night you could pick up Chicago, a big thrill.

The question is, how do we measure inflation? Is it the cost of a hamburger, or the quality of life? Is a car today the equivalent of a car in 1960? Most appliances are probably cheaper and better today than fifty years ago. I know microwaves are. A ball point pen in 1955 cost about five dollars, and would not write over anything touched by a human hand. Have you ever seen a 1900's Sears catalogue? A comb cost fifteen dollars, a shovel twenty five. Does a two penny nail cost two pennies today?

Just a thought and it is still only a penny.

DRIVING

My children and ex-wives always made fun of my driving, too slow, too cautious. I guess I could step on it a little bit more. That way I could wait on the red light an extra fifteen seconds.

I've had three speeding tickets in forty seven years of driving. Two were in the first six months I had my license, both speed traps where the limit went from forty to twenty five for about two blocks, specifically placed to increase the local government's coffers. If I had known that flashing headlights in the middle of the day meant "speed trap ahead" I would only have received one. The third ticket was on the Rhode Island Expressway, a sixty MPH limit down to 30 MPH due to construction in the opposite direction. Five State troopers pulled as many cars over as possible, handed out tickets and then grabbed the next group of unlucky motorists. Not one car on that road was driving under 55. I was informed the lower limit was in force for the next twenty miles, and after receiving my summons tried to comply with the lower limit. After two miles and almost being rear ended several times by less enlightened motorists, I let the German in me go, and sped along with the rest of the sane world.

My son will tell you my greatest driving pet peeve is being "boxed in". This is where cars in front and along side drive at the exact speed, and you can't pass, or drop back to a safe following distance. This condition was exacerbated when my screaming "Don't F-ing box me in" was followed be giggling in the back seat.

This would really drive me bonkers, the backseat "he's touching me" crap. This is universal to all siblings bored with a long trip. It is really hard to drive with one hand while reaching back trying to smack three miniature

Mohammad Ali's. If I had it to do over, I would name one child Notme, so I could always know whom to blame for these car infractions.

Chris and Road Rage

Road rage is a common problem today. When I have a crazy behind me, tail gating and honking, I just pull over, stop, and let him pass. The best response to road rage I know came from my brother Chris.

Chris cut in front of someone, or some such infraction, and when we pulled up to a traffic light the offended motorist pulled up right beside us, we in the right turn lane, he in the straight ahead lane. This nut job was screaming invectives at Chris like nobody's business. Mother this, and mother that, I oughta do this and I oughta do that, etc etc.

As Chris was in the wrong, I expected him to offer an apology and be done with it. Not Chris! The future Judge waited until just before the light turned green, rolled down the window and asked this red face lunatic. "Excuse me, what is your name?" Flustered by the question the angry driver paused and then stammered, "Charlie". As, the light turned green, just before he made the right hand turn, Chris replied, "Well, FUCK YOU Charlie", and sped away...... We could hear his veins popping from two blocks away!

Let me offer a word of advice if you are ever pulled over by a State Trooper. These guys never know what to expect when they pull a motorist over. Don't make it hard on them! All troopers are at least six two, built out of chiseled granite, spit shined and crisp. In one hundred degrees, they still do not sweat. Back talking is really a bad idea (besides it will lead to heroin addiction). Have you license ready, both hands on the wheel, and speak when spoken to. They are always super polite; you need to be the same. Do not get your registration out of the glove compartment until asked. If he sees you reaching for the compartment before he asks, he is trained to be aware of a possible gun. Admit to nothing, but do not dispute anything. Chances are you will still get a summons, but it will probably be for doing 65 in a 60 MPH limit instead of the 75 you were probably doing. Big difference when it comes to points on your license and insurance rate increases.

CUTTING THE CHEESE

I hate to admit it, but the funniest thing I can think of is the fart. Even the name, fart, and the condition, flatulence, are funny. Before you judge, did you not laugh 'til you peed during the baked bean campfire scene in "Blazing Saddles"? Women almost never fart, and certainly never admit to it. The family dog gets blamed for everything. "Oh Rufus!!!".

Men revel in their gas, high fiving each other, and in college even experimenting with the lighted fart phenomenon. The back draft from this experiment occasionally sends a very embarrassed undergrad to the emergency room (CAUTION, improper use of this process MAY RESULT IN DEATH"). What grandchild hasn't giggled over Grandpa's pull my finger routine?

In my house growing up, farts were never openly recognized. Dad would occasionally rattle the walls with a blast, and nobody said a thing. The more embarrassing the situation, the funnier is the fart. Farts in Church or an elevator are particularly funny, though laughter must be held in until deemed appropriate.

Farts need not be loud to be funny. There is not a single person with a nose that is not familiar with the term "silent but deadly" or the accusatory "he who smelt it dealt it".

As a young boy, I was never more surprised or proud of my Uncle Jack than when he secretly played for me an underground record called "The Crepitation Contest". It was about a heavy weight farting contest. The Champion was the English Lord Windisphere; the challenger was Australian Paul Boomer.

The contest was narrated by a very proper Englishman. Every sound effect as the contestants gripped the "Fawting" pole had me in tears. The challenger won when though knocked down by a powerful "triple woopsie sizzler", the champion was disqualified for pooping his trunks.

Years later while going through some old reel-to-reel tapes that Dad discovered, we found "The Contest" in his collection. My staid father laughed to tears at the replay, and I found a new respect for Dad. "OH MILTON!" "Now Chriis."

Maybe it's just me, but then why is the "Whoopee Cushion" a novelty store classic?

CATALINA, SWIM TEST AND LI'L TOOT

When I was age five to eight, we lived in the hoity toity Los Angeles suburb of San Marino. I suppose we were wealthy, but as the only one of my friends without a swimming pool, I never felt we were more than middle class (if five year olds even thought of such things). Pop bought a thirty-two foot cabin cruiser, the Mable H, named for Mom's favorite aunt. It was a comfortable, sea-worthy craft, and when Pop could get both engines purring, made the one hour trip to Catalina Island in a little over three hours. The trip to this little piece of paradise was generally made with Dad hanging upside down under one engine or the other cursing and tinkering to keep it going.

Catalina was unbelievably beautiful. You could clearly see bottom from thirty feet. It was a giant aquarium with a plethora of beautiful fish, kelp, and sea life constantly in view. Jim and Dad would skin dive and we had halibut, abalone (tasty mollusks with unbelievably beautiful multi-colored, iridescent, shells which ended up as ash trays) and rock lobster. We ate really well.

My favorite part of our boat was the dingy, "Li'l Toot", eight feet long and powered by a one and a half horse Evinrude outboard. I was allowed to row Li'l Toot only if Jim or Chris was on board. I had many opportunities to do so and became quite an efficient oars man. Before Dad would let me take out the dingy on my own, I had to pass a swim test.

Parents in the 50's and 60's were way less worried about their children than parents of today. Perhaps it is because they were not bombarded with horror stories on the news, kids' pictures on milk cartons, and MAY RESULT IN DEATH warnings on everything from peanut butter to extension cords. An example of the more relaxed attitude of this generation was my friend Alfred's mom, Mrs. Morrison.

The Morrisons had about twelve kids. I could never keep count; they were just all over the place. One day while playing upstairs with Alf, a blood curdling scream came from the basement. "WAA Mom, Bobby hit me with a brick; he's trying to KILL ME." Mrs. Morrison opened the basement door and called out, "OK, but if I have to come down, there'd better be blood!" All crying came to a halt, and life went on in the Morrison House.

Back to the swim test. Dad decided that in order for me to take Li'l Toot out on my own, I had to swim across the lagoon, where we docked Mable H, and back, a distance of maybe forty yards. The lagoon was about ten feet deep, and all objects were invisible at a depth of about two and a half feet. I was six, and ready for the test. Dad sat on the back of Mable H, cocktail in hand and said "go for it." The test was pass or fail, pass and you can take out the dingy on your own, fail and "Oh well". Apparently if I drowned I would not be allowed to take out Li'l'Toot!

"Wait a minute, I knew you could do it, and Jim was ready to dive in if you started to falter!"

"Yes I was, plus you had those green Voit frog fins to help"

I know, but I was just five and the story is better my way for God sake!

"YES"

OH, sorry God, I was just talking to Dad and my brother.

"Well make it snappy, you're tying up the lines."

Ok, I'm done; I forgot about the fins, they did make it easier.

Pass I did! The next day, I was off on my own skippering my own vessel unescorted, at age six. I proceeded to row out of the lagoon into Balboa Harbor, and towards the inlet to the great Pacific. Half way across the harbor in almost no time, I decided perhaps I had gone far enough and headed back to the safety of our lagoon. The row back was not as fast as the row out. Apparently it is much easier to row with the wind and the tide, than it is to row against the wind and tide! I rowed back for almost an hour, and based on the shore line figured I had progressed about negative thirty yards.

Today's parents, if they even let a six year old row a boat on his own, would certainly never let him out of the lagoon. If gone missing, they would call out the police, the coast guard, and set search on their own. The headlines would read "Child Missing, Gone Adrift". Dad was apparently alarmed enough after an hour and a half to send out Jim with his friend's outboard boat to "Go find your brother". Find me he did, and after laughing at and teasing me a bit I was towed home, to no great relief, no great fan fare, only the suggestion that in the future I should start any trip rowing against the tide. I guess if you grow up during WWI, saw siblings and friends pass away from the flu and TB, suffered through the Great Depression, went through WWII, the Korean conflict, and knew other children crippled from polio, a small boy adrift in the middle of a busy harbor is no reason to panic.

My brothers loved Li'l Toot, and at age 11 and 13 were allowed to take her out under full power. With the one and a half HP Evinrude she could reach speeds of 4 knots, and with the tank topped off to the full one half gallon, would run for over an hour. At age seven, I was ready to operate Li'l Toot, with the engine, as long as Jim or Chris was with me.

I set out on my maiden voyage at the helm, wrapped in a life preserver which with some effort allowed me to actually move my arms. With Jim at the bow we were headed to explore a favorite deserted island in the Harbor which is now probably covered with condos. As we sped past the last dock in the lagoon, a friend of Jims waved, and Jim waved back.

Anxious to show off my skippering prowess, I decided to put the boat in reverse and back up so Jim could talk to his friend. It was a maneuver I had seen many times. Simply spin the engine 180 degrees and the boat was in reverse. Unfortunately, I never realized this procedure was only performed at a very slow speed. I spun the engine around at full throttle, and Li'l Toot flipped over like a coin. One moment Jim was on the bow waving, the next we were in the water with Lil Toot floating upside down, the precious Evinrude completely immersed in the salt water lagoon.

Dad took the engine apart, dried it out, cleaned it up, lubed it, tuned it, and it ran again, but it was never the same. Its power was gone; it sputtered and stalled when least expected. The engine was never the same, and I don't think Jim or Chris ever completely forgave me.

"I forgive you; besides it was a good story"

Thanks Jim.

KID'S GAMES

As kids, we were never bored. If we got bored Mom or Dad would find something for us to do. There was always a basement to be cleaned, or weeds to be pulled. Kids today have iPods, computers, Playstations, X Boxes, cell phones, cable TV, and every game or toy known to man, and they still get bored.

If it was nice out, we played outside. If it was raining we played Backgammon, Chess, Checkers, or card games. We played solitaire, spit in the ocean, gin rummy or hearts. We played battleship with graph paper, and yachtzee with five dice before those games were even "invented" by Parker Brothers.

Indoors we played knee football, tough on the knees, and lamps; "Chris Jim Joe!!" We played sock baseball and jammed a bent metal hanger with an old tee shirt as a net into a doorway to play sock basketball. The metal hangers with the card board inserts that came back from the cleaners were also perfect for bow and arrow target practice, or cowboy and Indian fights. Ten AA batteries and a golf ball and we had indoor bowling. Mom one time admitted that while cleaning up she often took some time out to shoot a few hoops or roll a few battery bowling lines.

Outside we played touch football and several variations of baseball. The biggest issue with outdoors play was keeping balls out of Mrs. Rosenthal's yard. Mrs. Rosenthal was fiercely protective of her flower beds and if a ball landed in her yard would rush out and snatch it up. She had quite a collection of spaldeens and wiffle balls!

One year Grandma Hagy gave us a football for Christmas–, not just any football, but a fifteen dollar genuine leather NFL football. When an errant pass landed in Mrs. Rosenthal's garden, she raced out of the house and picked up the ball. Previously, any ball in Mrs. Rosenthal's hands was considered lost. This was a fifteen dollar genuine leather NFL football. Chris leapt over the garden, snatched the ball away and said, "This one you can't have!"

Incensed, Mrs. Rosenthal called the house and got Dad. She gave Dad hell about his unruly children and how difficult it was to raise flowers. Dad listened patiently and then responded," Mrs. Rosenthal, I fully respect how you love your flowers, and I have tried to instill this respect in my sons. They have never before crossed your property (not with her looking anyway) but this is a special ball. You are trying to raise flowers. I am trying to raise three boys, and I assure you they are every bit as important to me as the flowers are to you. Mrs. Rosenthal, this conversation is over!" We did not hear from Mrs. Rosenthal again......Dad was the best!

The king of all outdoor games was wiffle ball.

THE GREAT GEORGE GARBAGEBOATWALK

NOTE: "The Great George Garbageboatwalk" story was written 25 years ago as a Christmas present to Chris. Chris liked it and submitted it to Sports Illustrated as a "Reminiscence" piece. It was promptly turned down by a Linda Verigan. What would a "Linda" know of wiffle ball and brothers? In keeping with my professed laziness, I am submitting the story again, intact. If this material ever gets published-PFFFFT to Linda (Who is still on the SI Staff) if not, "WHAT' ever".

The game of baseball takes on many shapes to kids with little space and lots of imagination. In the streets it becomes stickball and punchball. When the streets are too crowded, stepball prevails. In the backyards of suburbia, in the late fifties when the Yankees were kings, the ultimate form was wiffle ball.

The Wiffle ball is a small hollow plastic sphere with holes strategically positioned so that the slightest change in grip will produce a variety of inshoots, outshoots, risers and drops. The slight weight of the ball precludes the possibility of a broken window, and when struck with a bat it can be driven such a limited distance that the smallest yard can become Yankee Stadium.

A popular game for many in our neighborhood, my brother Chris, four years my senior and I developed wiffle ball into an art form. The rules were designed so that one person could form a team. We had three bases; first, third, and home. Second base was discarded as our yard was not wide enough to form a normal diamond. A fielded grounder thrown within three feet of a base and ahead of the runner was a putout. We allowed two outs to an at-bat. Any ball which did not at least reach the pitcher's mound was foul. There were no walks, no called strikes, (you were expected to swing at anything close) and three strikes you're out. There were never any arguments; tie goes to the runner and the rest of the rules were clear.

There was no left field in our Stadium, only left center. A right-handed pull-hitter was in danger of reaching the yard of the dreaded Mrs. Rosenthal. This became an automatic out due to the danger of Mrs. Rosenthal leaping out of nowhere to abscond with any ball which might land in her precious yard.

A ball hit over the hedge in center and into the Tully's yard was a homerun. A pop fly lofted over the telephone wire in short right field, our own pennant porch, was also a homer.

If a ball landed and stayed on the roof along the right field foul line it was an automatic out and the batter had to shinny up the drainpipe to retrieve the treasured 19 cents of plastic gold.

Our bat was a forerunner of modern equipment. We used a section of an aluminum shaft from an old spear gun. It was the first aluminum bat.

The actual game as my brother and I played it was of secondary importance. My brother was older and more skilled than I, and it was a foregone conclusion that he would score the most runs. The real game was in creating the illusion of a big league contest. Each team required its own special line-up.

Unlike other kids who assumed the personalities and line-ups of their favorite major league team, we had to invent our own players because we were both diehard Yankee fans and each refused to compete against his heroes. Inventing and developing players became one of the chief skills of "The Game."

We developed and acted out the persona of each "member" of our teams. Yankee P.A. man, Bob Sheppard, announced lineups, pinch hitters and pitching changes. Mel Allen called the play-by-play. Great fielding plays received a "how about that" and all homeruns were greeted with the obligatory "going going gone" that was Mel's trademark. We had bean ball wars, players were thrown out of the game for arguing, and all players were described as "one of the nicest fellahs off the field that you'd ever want to meet."

Each player on our squads had a particular skill and a unique personality. Any variance from these traits was strictly forbidden (an unspoken rule). The player's skill and personality was dictated by his name; much like professional wrestling at this time, Killer Kilwalski, Haystacks Calhoun, Gorgeous George....

For years the stars of Chris' team were Little Louie, a quick shortstop and clever punch-hitter, and Big Mike, a slow but powerful slugger. Louie was allowed to run fast to first base but had no power as he always choked halfway up the bat. Big Mike was a tremendous power-hitter but was so slow afoot he was a sure out on any grounder. Chris cleverly managed to sneak his favorite Yankee pitcher on the mound, Whitey Ford, by introducing a crafty right-hander by the name of Blacky Buick.

Other members of my brother's unbeaten team were Cyclone Sam, a speedster, Killer Klu, a slugger who rolled up his sleeves and assumed the stance of Ted Kluszewski, and Happy Harry, a utility fielder and team flake.

For the most part my club concentrated on speed. The outfielders were Hurricane Hank, Rapid Rupert, and Cheetah Chaz. Chokeup Charlie played shortstop, Lumbering Luke was my power-hitter, and catcher Stu Pid was my resident flake. To combat Blacky Buick I developed Flower Weekly, another crafty right-hander who threw a knuckler suspiciously like Yankee star Bud Dailey.

Every game new players were invented and brought up from the minors to meet specific situations. If they played well they stuck. If they struck out it was back to triple A. I tried numerous players and constantly juggled my lineup, but never could I beat the great Chris Allstars.

Most games did go down to the last inning, a result of Chris' manipulation to prevent "laughers" which made "The Game" dull. Manipulation of the game was of prime importance. The object was to give a glimmer of hope that my troops could possibly win, and at the same time force the Allstars to demonstrate their great skills in the clutch.

If Chris was in the middle of a big inning, he would kill the rally by sending up Killer Klu who generally struck out due to his tendency to take prodigious swings with his eyes shut. On the mound Blacky would help me back in a game by throwing his famed "elbow pitch" change-up. The elbow pitch was a weird lob which I was able to consistently hit, provided I could keep from breaking up laughing at the outrageous delivery with which it was thrown. If the game was still not close enough, Happy Harry would resort to his flakey fielding to tighten up the score. Harry would try to catch flies behind his back, in his pocket, or on a rebound off his head.

Once I was back in the game, the Allstars would finish it with a dramatic pinch hit homerun or by the superior pitching of the master, Blacky Buick. The results were always the same. Mel Allen would announce a typical exciting finish. "Bottom of the ninth, 6-4 Chris ahead, one out and the bases are jammed. Gripping the old aluminum comes Lumbering Luke to the plate. Luke is a real slugger who could ice this game up with one swing. Blacky goes into his windup, delivers the pitch...swing and a miss on a wicked inshoot! Blacky remembers the third inning when Luke pounded an elbow pitch over the hedge in center and you can bet the chairman of the board won't make that mistake again. Here comes the pitch….swing and a pop-up to short. Little Louie is under it, he pounds his palm, and the ballgame is over."

Although I never beat the Allstars, I did achieve the next best thing in the summer of 1959. I invented a ballplayer that Chris fell in love with and had to have on his own team.

One of Chris' favorite players was Yankee great, Moose Skowrun. The "Moose", Big Bill, Chris loved him, but as with most of his heroes he could not find a way to slip him into his lineup.

One warm July afternoon, Mel Allen announced a pinch hitter for the Joes. "Now batting, up from Columbus, is the latest sensation, first baseman, number 14, Big George Garbageboatwalk." "Time out", Chris protested, "what the Hell kind of name is Garbageboatwalk?" "What is a scow", I responded and without waiting for an answer, "it's a garbage boat, "and" I hastened to elaborate, "The opposite of run is walk. Scow-run, Garbageboatwalk, it fits." I loved it and though he said nothing, I knew Chris loved it also.

So determined was I that Garbageboatwalk be a success, I distained the left-handed stance we normally assumed to avoid the crazy lady in leftfield, and made and made "Big George" a right-hander, my natural stance. As much as I wanted George to be a star, my brother wanted him on his team. Unbeknownst to me he plotted a course of action which would set up the first trade and biggest steal in wiffle ball history.

From the outset Chris mocked the name and refused to acknowledge my ingenuity. For weeks, every time Garbageboatwalk stepped up to the plate he saw only the best inshoots and drops which Blacky could muster. The great Buick threw no elbow pitches and his risers had a little something extra on them.

George was an immediate flop. Mel began to refer to him as "the biggest disappointment in wiffle ball history." Hitless in ten games and with eighteen strikeouts, I was ready to give up on "Big George". It was then that Chris struck. "Tell you what", he offered casually, "I'll trade you even up, Little Louie for Garbageboatwalk."

The deal was made. I had to do it. An established star for the "biggest disappointment in wiffle ball history" could not be passed up. The first trade in wiffle ball history was sealed, and like the Yankee purchase of Babe Ruth it changed the face of "The Game".

Little Louie was damaged goods. The veteran had lost a step, his hands were not as sure, and his bat was not as quick as it was in his Allstar days. Meanwhile, George Garbageboatwalk became the greatest hitter in all of wiffle ball! His first five times up as an Allstar he pounded out tremendous home-runs. George batted over .700 for the rest of the year, and he averaged one round-tripper for every three times at bat.

The ultimate manipulation became a Garbageboatwalk blast in the ninth. It was the cruelest humiliation over which I had no control. Flower invented new pitches, threw bean balls, and refused to throw the ball over the plate. It did not matter; George was just too great. He was far better than my old nemesis, Big Mike who Flower could occasionally get out.

I dreaded Garbageboatwalk's every at bat. The joy of the game was over for me. It was devastating to face the "greatest hitter in wiffle ball history and know he was once my property. Every time up the introduction was the same. In the best imitation of Yankee PA Bob Sheppard, Chris would drone, "Now batting ing ing number fourteen een een the first baseman and onetime property of the Joes, the Great George Garbageboatwalk alk alk!"

1959 was the last season of Wiffle ball for my brother and me. Chris got his driver's license and became too grown up for his kid brother and a silly game. "The Game" and the "Great One" were soon forgotten. Chris went to college, and then to law school. Our folks moved from Long Island to New Jersey, and later retired to the Eastern Shore of Maryland. Chris married, took up law practice in Atlanta, and became father to two sons. I graduated from college, married, and became a Jersey-to-NYC commuter. My wife and I had three children, a girl and two boys.

Years later, during a summer reunion at our parent's new home, we stumbled upon the old aluminum bat. We began to reminisce on the way we used to play "The Game". "They just don't make players like Blacky Buick or Cheetah Chaz today" Chris asserted.

He did not mention George, "Guilt", I thought to myself, "he knows he stole him. Now it's like it never happened."

I wanted to say something about Garbageboatwalk as some wounds never heal. I decided to let it slide, let bygones be bygones. Instead I followed up on his thought. "Probably have a relief pitcher today named Cocaine Carl," I joked. "Yeah" Chris followed, "with a peculiar habit of first going to the rosin bag and then to his nose in tough situations." "Or Millionaire Mike", I continued, "a DH with special designer shoes and Gucci batting gloves who spends most his time on the dugout phone talking to his stock broker."

We continued on this vein for some time when Chris issued a challenge. It would be he and his two boys versus me and mine. I accepted but suggested we play the game straight so as not to ruin our image with the boys. "Yeah", Chris agreed, "God forbid they find out we used to be kids too."

And so we purchased a new 69 cent wiffle ball, established ground rules, explained the game to the boys, and play began.

Three against three, Chris and I both full grown; he no longer had the obvious advantage of strength and coordination. In fact age was now to my advantage and I had my first real chance to actually defeat the Allstars. As agreed upon we did not play with the old childish flair. There was no play-by-play announcing, and we assumed no alter egos at bat. On the mound, though unnamed, the pitchers' deliveries were unmistakably those of Blacky Buick and Flower Weekly.

It was a low scoring, uneventful game as the boys were usually easy outs. Going into the bottom of the ninth my team held a 6-5 lead over the Allstars. Little Chris, my brother's oldest, popped out and with Grant, his youngest, at bat I felt my first victory was at hand. Grant managed a bloop single, but I still felt in control when my greatest fear was realized.

As Chris strode to the plate, I recognized a familiar grin on his face. He underwent a strange transformation. His 5'9" slightly paunchy frame seemed to grow to 6'2" 210 pounds of steel. Muscles bulged and a vein in his now 17" neck started pulsating. Aluminum was flaking off the bat under his now powerful grip. Nothing was said, but in my head I heard the familiar Bob Sheppard voice, "Now batting ing ing, number fourteen een een, first baseman and one time property of the opposition on on……"

A lump formed in the pit of my stomach. If guilt had caused Chris to forget, competition and the threat of his first loss had revived his memory. The outcome of "The Game" was once again a foregone conclusion.

The Great George Garbageboatwalk was coming to bat!

FOOD

I love food. I am not a gourmet by any stretch of the imagination, but I love food. I guess I am basically a meat and potatoes guy, probably because Mom was a meat and potatoes kind of cook. Growing up I thought Mom was a great cook, and I still list Mac and Cheese as one of my favorite dishes. I think everyone thinks their Mom was a great cook. Turns out I was wrong. I like anything with bacon, and or butter. I love corn on the cob and lobster, mostly as they are excellent venues for butter.

I have actually learned to eat artichoke hearts, brussels sprouts and asparagus. As a child, asparagus looked like green turds, and made me gag. It was the one food my parents forced me to eat (sorry about the lima bean Mike), a big mistake as it took years for me to finally actually eat new foods voluntarily.

Forcing kids to eat different foods is a big mistake. Kids have a limited palate, and no incentive to change. Peanut butter and jelly is delicious. What motive do kids have to try anything else! HUNGER! Hunger is the best incentive. Don't fight with kids over what to eat. Give them what you eat, and let nature take its course. If they don't eat the peas, so be it. If they don't eat anything, they will eventually.

Eating should not be a battle. Try to serve at least something you know your children like. Don't serve all new stuff, and gradually introduce different foods. The worst thing you can do is prepare two meals, one for you and one for the children. Like everything else with children, parents spend way too much time worrying about what and how kids eat. I swear if experts found children needed to inhale and exhale 22 times a minute, some parents would follow their kids around with a stop watch and tell them when to breathe.

If children will not try different foods at home, take them out to eat. Children invariably choose to try new foods at a restaurant. They look for the most expensive item on the menu, and that is what they have to have.

My Dad solved this problem when we moved from California back to Long Island in 1955. He allocated fifty dollars to each of us with the caveat that when we ran out of money, we ran out of food, and conversely whatever money we did not spend we could keep. Seven days on the road, breakfast, lunch and dinner, and none of us spent over thirty dollars. Dad was no dope.

Why is prime rib so expensive in the supermarket and relatively inexpensive at a restaurant? Why is salmon relatively inexpensive in the supermarket and expensive at a restaurant?

Scallops wrapped in bacon sounds delicious. Why can't anyone cook the damn bacon!

Don't order seafood at a steak house, or at any restaurant more than 200 miles from the ocean.

The New York tri state area makes the best pizza in the world, yet Pizza Hut and Dominos Pizza fast food chains thrive. If you want good pizza, get it at Vinnie's or Roberto's for God sake!

Growing up, we never had pizza; in our house the only ethnic food served was spaghetti and meatballs, or occasionally Chinese takeout. The only thing I knew about pizza is that it was what made my brothers throw up when they came home late on Saturday nights. Apparently several pitchers of beer were also involved. I don't think Dad was ever really fooled. Whenever my brothers got "sick" on Saturday night, he always got religion and woke everyone up early for church on Sunday.

Even though pizza always smelled so good, I never tried it as I didn't want to get sick. The first time I ever ate pizza was in college. I found that several pitchers of beer usually made me sick anyway so I got real brave and tried a slice. Oh my God! I ordered pizza for the next three days.

What is it about Chinese food that makes you eat so fast? When I eat Chinese, even though it comes in very healthy portions, I eat like someone is going to come and take it away. Probably it is just me.

What is Duck Sauce? I use it on everything Chinese except duck. Is it a sauce for duck, or was it invented by a man named Duc? Duc's sauce? Speaking of ducks, is it Duck tape or Duct tape? It is good on everything but air ducts. I never tried it on ducks.

Why do people put parmesan cheese on food? That crap smells like vomit! In college we used to combine it with vegetable soup as a gag to simulate throw up. (By the way, when someone tells you what they used to do in college, it generally means they did it once.) We used to sneak into the movies by entering through the exit when the last show was over; did it once. We used to fire veal cutlets (known as elephant scabs) at the Chi Phi house with a surgical tube sling shot; did it once.

There were so many delicious foods that I never tried, why did I eat and like creamed chip beef on toast?

What the Hell is mince meat? Don't tell me, it sounds disgusting, but I love it!

Sloppiest food to eat: steamed crabs.

Food which would never have been eaten if not for alcohol and or gambling: raw oysters, clams, mushrooms or liver.

Foods I will never try; sushi, pickles, sauerkraut, or raw onions. I've gone this far. Why spoil my record?

RT - All you ladies trying the internet dating thing; if you use the line "It's not the breaths you take in life, but the times in life that take your breath away", you should expect to meet a lot of very neat men with good fashion sense, clean apartments and they will clap without cupping their hands. They will also notice when you change your hairdo.

PSYCHICS

Here is a real bull shit bunch of charlatans! If they can tell the future, why aren't they in the stock market instead of ripping people off? "The letter "B" keeps coming to me; do you know anyone whose name begins with "B"? Bill, Barry, Betty, Bob?" "Why yes, my brother-in-law's name is Bob!" "I feel sickness, or death. Does this make any sense to you?" "Well his Mother passed on about three years ago." "Yes, I see clearly now. Tell Bob his Mother is fine, and is looking down on him." "Oh thank you, that is so good to hear, you are amazing!"………PAHLEEZE!!

I have a friend who knows a "professional" Psychic. She tells me he has been hitting on her for a year, takes her out to dinner on a monthly basis, but she only wants to be friends. Get a grip dude, you're a Psychic. It ain't going to happen!

Matt was all into this John Edwards guy and talking to the dead. I told him when I am gone, see a psychic and ask about me. If he mentions the phrase "The blue moon is really green (the real phrase is still between him and me) then you'll know it is for real!" Know what the little bastard tells me? "Gee Dad, I can hardly wait!"

RT - Why are there eighty different concoctions advertized and sold for acid indigestion and heartburn when a teaspoon of baking soda and water works just fine?

HEALTH CARE

Another subject I know very little about, but I do have opinions!

Why is health care so expensive today? Well maybe because they can do stuff for you. In the fifties if you came down with something bad all the doctor had for you was an estimate! It was very cheap to die in the old days.

With insurance paying for just about everything, people see the doctor for just about anything. It costs money for a doctor to tell you that you have a severe throat and sinus infection. It was very cheap for Mom to tell you that you have a sore throat and a cold. When Moms used to stay at home there was a consortium of Dr. Moms. When your child came down with something, there was a Mom whose child had the same thing and could tell you just how to treat the ailment.

As kids we almost never went to the doctor because insurance only covered the big stuff. When I was nine, we were on vacation at the shore for a month (well Dad wasn't; he almost never took off from work). Due to my horrible eating habits, I had iron deficiency anemia. For two weeks I woke up every day with a pillow soaked in blood from a nose bleed. Was Mom worried? "When we get back home", she fretted, "we may have to see a doctor about this."

Doctors are so worried about malpractice suits they test you for everything even if their training tells them these tests are not necessary. Very expensive. Doctors cannot even give you their best advice for fear of a lawsuit. If a pregnant woman asks if she can have an occasional glass of wine, the advice is absolutely not! Is a glass of wine OK? Probably, but when the same lady drinks a half bottle of scotch every day and sues because the baby had fetal alcohol problems, she is going to say she only had an occasional glass of wine and the doctor said that was OK. Why would any doctor take that chance? Lucy smoked and drank on TV, and little Ricky was just fine.

When things are free, they will be in great demand, and scarce. Hospitals are required to treat everyone who comes to the Emergency Room regardless of the patient's ability to pay. It is the right thing to do, but irritating when you go in with a substantial injury and have to wait while some clown gets a splinter removed from his finger, and then gets sent home with a free supply of iodine, Tylenol and bandages.

Free health care is a great idea, and there are surely some improvements which can be made in our system, but at what cost? Sorry, but the best doctors will always go to those that can afford them. Why else would the best doctors become the best doctors? There will never be equality of care unless the care is equally lousy.

I would love to play golf at the best courses in the country, but I can't afford it. If golf courses were all free, the only way to get a tee time on the good courses would be to slip a few bucks to the starter. Even the public courses we have today would become so overcrowded there would be a many weeks wait to play. Why would free health care be any different?

Why should insurance pay for a normal birth. Having a baby is your choice, if you can't afford the hospital and the doctor, don't get pregnant. I had three children who were not covered by my insurance, and it took me years to finally pay all the bills. My choice. If we get government health insurance, it should be limited coverage, and it needs to cost something. Almost everybody in this country has TVs, cell phones, air conditioning and other luxuries not available years ago. Everyone should have to pay something for health care, and sorry, but someone has to see the guy who graduated last in his class. Yes there needs to be exceptions, but if you have to see a doctor, "there'd better be blood!"

RT - If man is so smart, why did it take so long to invent a folding beach chair that would not pinch your fingers?

IMAGINE

How did John Lennon's "Imagine" become the utopian anthem for my generation and those who followed? Is it just me or are the lyrics to this song anti-God, anti-capitalist, drop everything and have a good time, and everyone will live in peace, harmony, equality, and poverty? Nothing to fear, nothing to look forward to, no possessions, no God, no hate, no war, no hope, no love, just nothing! Imagine.

Imagine there's no Heaven	(Why is that a comforting thought?)
It's easy if you try	
No hell below us	(No repercussions for bad behavior?)
Above us only sky	
Imagine all the people	
Living for today	(Sex drugs and rock and roll)
Imagine there's no countries	(Yea, that will work)
It isn't hard to do	
Nothing to kill or die for	(Anything to live for?)
And no religion too	(Ever been in a fox hole?)
Imagine all the people	
Living life in peace	(Got to all be on drugs)
You may say that I'm a dreamer	
But I'm not the only one	
I hope someday you'll join us	
And the world will be as one	
Imagine no possessions	(Can I at least have a tent, or a toilet?)
I wonder if you can	
No need for greed or hunger	(Hunger? Can we possess food?)
A brotherhood of man	(???)

Imagine all the people
Sharing all the world   (Share what, no possessions remember?)

You may say that I'm a dreamer
But I'm not the only one
I hope someday you'll join us
And the world will live as one

I'm pretty sure this was the theme song for the Manson Family. Everyone thinks this is the greatest song ever written. Whenever there is a tragedy or a war, or a terrorist act, everyone plays this song and sighs....Oh, Imagine! Imagine! Sigh!

Imagine all the Lemmings,
marching off the cliff,
Imagine drink the Kool Aid,
I think you get the drift,
Imagine everybody,
doing what THEY say

You may say I'm a blasphemer
But that's not how it should be done
Why not just join us
And the world may not be so dumb

Ahhhh sigh.... IMAGINE. Just because the song sounds nice and was written by a Beatle, READ THE LYRICS!! This is not about utopia; it is from a drug addled mind that thinks the way to get rid of bad shit is to get rid of EVERY-THING!! Sigh.... Imagine
Well it is a nice song, so I imagine new lyrics

IMAGINE

Imagine there's a Heaven
Where good people get to go
A Hell below us
Which Bad ones will soon know
Imagine all the people
Living in this way

You may say I'm a blasphemer
But I'm not the only one
Why don't you join us
And the world won't be so dumb

Imagine there are no Liberals
It's easy if you try
No commies, fascists or dictators

It's their way or you die
Imagine all the people
Living with hope and free

You may say I'm a blasphemer
It could just be me
Why not try and join us
And maybe we will see

Imagine that your country
Remains as number one
Freedom to be successful
Possessions can be fun
Imagine everybody
With ethics and morals

You may say I'm a blasphemer
But I'm not the only one
Try honesty and hard work
And the world will not be so dumb

Is it really just ME??

2001 A SPACE ODYSSEY

As long as I'm attacking a musical icon, let's take a shot at the greatest movie of my time "2001 A Space Odyssey" "You have to see this movie, it's fantastic, genius, ahead of its time…" OK, I went to see it.

duh, duh, Duh…. DUMB DUMB, dumb dumb dumb dumb; dumb dumb dumb dumb, duh, duh, Duh, DUMB DUMBER.

I did not understand one bit of this movie! Monkeys dancing, Hal computing, what the FUCK!! I left this movie shaking my head, not a clue. "Wasn't that great? The symbolism, the cinematography, it's just fantastic!" "I don't get it", I replied.

"Really, you're kidding right, no? Wow and I thought you were smart!"

I've never found any one to explain; only "if you don't know I can't explain it to you" responses.

If this movie is so damn great, why has it not been rereleased? When have you ever seen it on TV? Who do you know owns the DVD? When did you last see it? Come on; admit it. This movie sucked! Or, Imagine all the lemmings, marching off the cliff……

It's probably just me.

DANGEROUS PHRASES

Here are the three most destructive argument enders of which I know, especially when unleashed by someone in a position of power. No matter how powerful the argument, these retorts will end the conversation:

"If it ain't broke, don't fix it!" This one is a killer. Come up with a new idea to vastly improve a product or process, carefully explain the benefits, show cost savings, everyone is almost on board, and some head of something or other whose entire position relies on not changing anything, stands up and like the wise old sage states, "Gentlemen, it all sounds very nice, but I say if it ain't broke, don't fix it!"

"Yes men" respond as one "Oh good one JB, if it ain't broke don't fix it", "Wise words JB", "What were we even thinking JB", "nothing wrong with the horse and buggy JB!" You fucking idiot JB.

Xerox ran a billion dollar think tank, invented work station file sharing, a windows type environment, and envisioned a paperless workplace. What happened to it? I'm guessing some genius in power got up and said "Gentlemen may I remind you we are in the copier business and you want to create a paperless environment?" "If it ain't broke, don't fix it!"......... It's all yours Mr. Gates.

"You know, it's a slippery slope" This is another saved for putting the kibosh on any attempt to make a change. It infers give in just a little and down the slope we will slip to catastrophe.

Like, "gee Your Highness, maybe we should let property owners actually vote on policies." "Well that's a slippery slope. Next thing peasants, women and

Negroes will be voting and bang.... Freedom." "Oh yea, good point, sorry I brought it up."

"If it costs a Billion dollars and saves one life, it's worth it." How do you dispute this one and not sound like a complete money hungry bastard? How many wasteful laws have been passed because of this humanitarian sounding comment? Here is my response, "Whose life are we spending one billion to save? Charles Manson, the next Adolph Hitler, who? While we save that life, how many jobs are lost due to revenue rerouting? What poor slob will blow his brains out because tax increases cause him to lose his house? No one wants to put a price tag on human life, but I'm pretty sure for one billion dollars we could do a lot better than save one life!

Could we just analyze new ideas on their merits, maybe even think a little bit before we make decisions based on these wise sounding one liners?

That's all I'm saying.

ALCOHOL

By all standards, I have to admit, I am an alcoholic. I come from a long line of alcoholics. Grandma and Grandpa, and most of my Aunts and Uncles were alcoholics. Not hide the bottle, have a few snorts for breakfast or lunch, slur your words and staggering Foster Brooks kind of drunks, but alcoholics none the less.

I remember, as a kid, cocktail hour for my relatives started at five. Dinner was at seven. You do the math. There was no fighting, no crazy stunts, but everyone had a rip roaring good time, every night. It never seemed bad to me. Drinks were pleasant sounding concoctions. "I'll have another highball". "Make mine a stinger." There were no sloe gin fizzes, or pink ladies. A highball was whiskey over ice (Before bed time, a high ball became a Mist). A stinger was vodka chilled with a hint of crème de menthe. Several of these drinks would put the average person on his butt, but my relatives seemed to be just fine and ready for dinner at seven. After dinner perhaps another highball would be nice, and before bedtime perhaps just a nightcap. Now all my relatives were productive citizens, wonderful fun people. Drinking was at home, no driving, and no one was hurt. If there is such a thing as social alcoholics, that would describe this crew.

Not a good thing, I'm just saying.

At about age twelve, I asked Grandpa what vodka tasted like. He poured me several fingers worth into a glass and encouraged me to "see for yourself." Downing the glass in one gulp, my eyes popped out and my throat visibly burned, as Grandapa laughed to tears. It was several minutes before I could even speak.

"OH MILTON"!

My next real drink did not come until college.

Mom and Dad did not drink very much. They would nurse no more than two drinks during "Cocktail Hour", and did so mostly out of peer pressure. I only saw my Dad under the weather once. Late one Saturday night I heard a small commotion in the garage. It was Mom trying to help Dad out of the car and into the house. She waved me away, not wanting me to see Dad in this condition. I assumed at the time that Dad had had a bad slice of pizza. I do remember that was one Sunday when everyone got to sleep in!

Mom was an alcoholic by some standards. She had a beer every day at five o'clock. She called it her five o'clock beer. She did not need a clock. When she wanted her beer, she would say. "It must be five o'clock". She was seldom off by more than five minutes. I was generally the one to fetch this five o'clock beer, and was rewarded with the first sip. The first sip is the best sip. Miller High Life was the brand, and to this day, though not a beer drinker, I enjoy an occasional taste of the High Life. Other brands do not do it for me.

Grandma Gus liked to drink, but she could not hold her liquor. When she had too much, crazy went to the next level. As a result, Dad was always sure to make the second or third drink for her.

"Jim, isn't this drink weak?"

"No Gusta, it's just fine. I mixed it myself."

"It seems weak".

"It's fine. The second drink always seems a little weak".

Well they always did when Dad made them for Grandma Gus!

Banned From Bermuda

I did get a little tipsy with Dad about three years before he passed, gin and tonic around a bar-b-q turning the chicken. Everyone should get a little pie eyed with their Dad just once. He told me how he and Uncle Tom were once banned from Bermuda for life because they were caught running those little scooters up and down the local airport runway. Uncle Tom should not have been allowed to ride a scooter sober. He had a wandering eye condition which for a driver's license had him labeled as legally blind.

"Hey, it was your Dad's idea"

That's what I thought Uncle Tom.

I'm not sure when this event took place, It was well before computers as Dad did go back to Bermuda several times. I think it must have been after an ocean race to Bermuda before the War, and Dad and Uncle Tom probably had reason to let off steam. This was a race in which Uncle Tom sailed an old cheap boat which probably should never have left the harbor. (Story has it that the next year they put a hole in the hull with a paint brush, so bad was the dry rot.)

They had no GPS, and apparently no radio in this race, and two weeks after the first boat finished, Dad and Uncle Tom were reported missing, and probably lost at sea. They were never lost, just really slow. When they finished the race, I'm sure they were relieved to report that stories of their demise were greatly exaggerated.

I like a nice glass of wine. I am not a connoisseur by any stretch of the imagination. I have my personal wine index. I judge wine by three criteria. Taste, cost, and how I feel in the morning. If it tastes good, and I have a headache in the morning, it was swill at any cost! Any wine over twenty dollars a bottle cannot taste good enough to pass my index.

I do not get the cork testing, decanting, sniffing, swirling, and swooshing in the mouth. "I detect a hint of peach, a little peppery, and a nice oakiness." Pahleeze! Oak taste? Yeeech! You want peppery, add pepper! Peach, I never taste the peach. How do you get peach? It all tastes like grape to me! Hmmmm what is it made of? Must just be me.

Ever see anyone sniff, swirl and swish Hawaiian Punch? "Is that strawberry, lime, and just a hint of guava? Come on, it tastes good or it doesn't!

Why do people try and push expensive single malt scotch. "Oh, this is so good, once you acquire a taste you won't be able to drink anything else." I am perfectly happy with Dewers or a lesser scotch at one third the price. Why would I want to acquire a taste for something I can't afford?

All right, it's just me.

My abuse of alcohol was basically a means of getting to sleep. When I had insomnia, I found a glass or two of scotch would help me relax. Eventually I had insomnia a lot!

I almost never drove impaired, and if I did, and I'm not proud of this, I was a very good drunk driver. Not a good driver, but a good drunk driver. I was not one to feel my oats and step on the accelerator, but recognized my condition and drove well below the speed limit. I was lucky to have never had an accident. I learned not to press my luck, and switched to cola at a party well before having to drive.

In college, we made frequent trips to Jack's, a little known no neon signed bar about ten miles of sparsely traveled country road off campus. The only proof of age which Jack required was the ten cents it costs for a six ounce glass of beer. We brought a lot of dimes. After most nights of revelry, we would stupidly limp slowly home along the empty road at a somewhat safe speed. One night we were forced to return packed seven deep into "Fast Freddy" James' four seat fast back corvette. Three in the front, four in the back like sardines. I could not even see out, but heard the front passengers exhort Freddy to step on it. "Fifty, sixty, come on Freddy, you can do seventy".

We somehow made it back, but there is a fine line between a future funny reunion story and a tragic front page headline.

I am pleased to report that I no longer need a cure for insomnia. I may have an occasional glass of wine, or scotch with dinner, but my drinking is no longer a regular event. It seems that what once as a young man improved romantic performance eliminates it as you get older. This is an easy choice.

RT - Why are there three handicap parking spaces (always empty) at my gym? I don't really care. Just a head scratcher.

SUMMER JOBS

People today complain about illegal immigration, and the claim is that these immigrants are taking the jobs that Americans will not take. Got to side with the Libs on this one, at least from what I see. Young Mexicans, illegal or not, seem to take most of the low skill labor, like cutting grass, and bussing tables, which used to be taken by teenagers, part time or as summer jobs. Today's young people are apparently above these jobs, choosing jobs which will someday lead to greater opportunity, or to not work at all. When I was a teen, I remember kids bragging and rejoicing when they landed a job bussing tables at the local restaurant. And some of these kids were rich!

Chris painted houses, and one summer, three years from entering Harvard Law School, worked spraying weeds and trees all over New Jersey, to prevent growth under the miles of power lines which cross the state. What he sprayed I don't know, (probably agent orange), but it smelled like Hell, and Chris was not allowed in the house until he stripped, threw his clothes in the wash (or away), and he then ran straight to the shower. It was truly a dirty job. I don't see young people taking these types of jobs today.

I painted houses (not very well, so not very often), dug holes for underground sprinkler systems, moved furniture, and worked the cash register at a mini golf course. The worst job I ever held was summer after my freshman year in college.

GREAT EASTERN MILLS

I was the box boy at Great Eastern Mills, a now defunct sell everything store similar to Target today. I worked for Harry, the custodian. My main job was to push around a large cart, and collect empty boxes to be burned in the incinerator. The burning was Harry's job. Harry had a lot of class. About forty five, going on seventy, he was a man of few, make that no, words. He did grunt from time to time. Harry always had a cigar, and when smoked to a nub, he would stuff the remaining spit soaked hunk of brown crap into a pipe, and finish every last bit of tobacco. Harry did not need a rest room. When needed, he would simply pee into the incinerator. The job paid minimum wage, $1.15 an hour. There was a ten minute break in the morning and afternoon, and thirty minutes for lunch.

On my first day of work, while pushing my cart, I heard my name called by a sweet female voice. Bing Bing, "Joe Hagy please, Joe Hagy". Bing Bing, "Joe Hagy please, Joe Hagy". I had often heard this Bing Bing call in finer department stores, and had always thought the person being paged must be very important. I sought a sales person, "That's me, what do I do?" Pointing to a phone on the wall, "Pick it up." Bing Bing, "Joe Hagy please Joe Hagy." I grabbed the phone, somehow feeling very important, "Hagy here." The other end responded in a very gruff, not sweet, not female voice, "Yea, listen Hagy, some kid just blew chunks in the luncheonette. Get over there with a mop and bucket right away and take care of it!" ......Bing Bing, "Joe Hagy please Joe Hagy". So much for feeling important.

I worked at Great Eastern Mills for exactly one week. I had the opportunity to take a house painting job, and after a week as the lowest totem on the pole, I was anxious to quit and pick up my $36 pay check after my final day. Pushing my cart through the aisles, un-showered and unshaven, I'm sure I was a sight to behold, or smelled.

I encountered a pocketbook sale which had attracted many a thrifty shopper digging through a bin of bargains. There was little room to pass, and as I tried to slip my cart past the shopping frenzy I barely touched the elbow of a particularly aggressive bargain hunter. "You idiot, you stupid stupid idiot", she shrieked, "you stupid idiot, why don't you watch where you're going?"

I think everyone can think of a time when they wish they did or said something but did not think of it until about twenty minutes later. This was the one time when I reacted instantly. With my best frightened and stupid stare, I responded in a retard voice, "Ahhm towwy laadee." The aggressive lady's venom turned to horror and pity for picking on such a poor soul. I continued on my way just pushing my cart, trying with all my might not to bust a gut from laughing at the look on her face. I hope she felt like shit.

Summer jobs were hard to find.

RT - Why do left handed athletes seem to throw the biggest curve balls in baseball, the biggest hooks in bowling, and put the most spin on serves in tennis? I think the difference is that all major organs, heart, liver, kidney and such are on the left hand side of the body. This weight distribution difference works to the left hander's advantage, and to the right hander's disadvantage.

I'm retired, I have lots of time!

PETS

There are three acceptable types of pets: dogs, cats, and birds. Rodents, reptiles, or insects are not pets. These are creatures which if you left the cage open would try to escape to the wild to boil, freeze, or be eaten. They would rather die than stay with you. This is even though you give them guaranteed food and shelter. These animals hate you; they cannot be real pets. Fish won't generally try to escape, but they are decorations, not pets.

Dogs, cats, and birds; anything else is a captive creature and could never be a member of the family. A real pet is a member of the family, usually the lowest member, but a member none the less.

CHARLIE BIRD

I would not have included birds as genuine pets if it were not for "Charlie Bird". Charlie Bird was Mom's parakeet. He was definitely one cool bird. Charlie Bird was free to roam the house most of the time. Generally he would fly from mirror to mirror to preen and admire himself. He was one handsome bird. The other place you could find Charlie Bird was perched on Mom's shoulder, beak to her mouth, as he listened and learned that month's new word or phrase. Charlie had over one hundred phrases which he would randomly utter from time to time, except in the morning when he would recite every phrase he knew from beginning to end, all in the order Mom taught him.

If we needed to get Charlie Bird back to his cage, you only had to squeeze his favorite squeaky toy which was by his perch. Charlie Bird would answer the call instantly, climb in his cage and protect his toy. Charlie Bird loved to play with his various toys. Charlie Bird loved people. He had no interest in escaping his free shelter and always full trays of seed and water.

One phrase I had Mom teach Charlie Bird was the pirate parrot traditional "Awk Awk pieces of eight." In my mind Charlie Bird would perch on your shoulder and holler "Awk Awk, piecesofeight" like a pirate's parrot. Mom, God bless her, though she knew deep down a parakeet would simply copy any noise he heard repeated enough, was intent to teach all phrases slowly and with perfect diction. This bird would imitate a spoon dropping if you did it enough, but Mom always wanted to make sure people could understand Charlie Bird.

The result of her training is that when I came home from school for Winter break, there was Charlie Bird perched on Mom's shoulder proudly repeating his newly learned phrase, "A a w k   A a w k,   p i e c e s   o f   e i g h t", slowly and with perfect Mom diction. He sounded like one wimpy pirate parrot!

Charlie Bird was cool, and Mom was a PIP!

I don't really like cats, but I do respect them. Cats are ideal pets for little old ladies and those who just want some occasional company without any real effort or commitment required. People don't own cats; they exist with them. Cats are independent. They will stick around because it is convenient shelter and food, but if you piss them off, they will be gone and simply live in the wild, or meow at someone else's door until they find a new partner more to their liking.

Cats can survive in the wild unlike other true pets. Cats like to kill and are very good at it. If need be they will also eat what they kill. If they like you, they will kill because they like to kill, and leave their conquest at your door for you to admire. Cats will come when called, if they want to. Cats will let you pet and stroke them, if they are in the mood. If the house is on fire, cats will find a way out; you are on your own.

I keep hearing from people, and ads on TV, that cats are finicky eaters. If they don't like what you give them, they will not eat. This would annoy me no end. I don't need a pet that I have to beg to have them feed themselves, and I'm damn sure not going to buy that gourmet cat food that I believe is really made for old people living on a fixed income. I don't think cats are really finicky about what they eat; I think they just have a hard time eating something that they didn't get to kill. I bet that if you put a can of cat food on a roller skate and pushed it down the hallway, the finicky cat would pounce on it and eat it no problem.

One good thing about cats, they pee and poop on their own in a litter box conveniently left in the bathroom. One bad thing about cats, when you use the bathroom there is a litter box full of cat pee and poop.

The best thing about cats is if you have a cat, you will not have mice.

Dogs are the best of the true pets. Dogs are pack animals, and are very happy to be part of your pack. They want to please you; they will come when called and do tricks for your amusement. Try to get a cat to roll over, or meow on command; not even for a bribe. If your house is on fire, a dog will make sure everyone in his pack is awake and safely out.

The right breed of dog can be taught to do just about anything to help its owner. They can flush and retrieve birds for a hunter; they will protect you from intruders, pull a cart, rescue you from an avalanche, and make sure that the mailman will leave every day after he delivers the mail. Have you ever heard of a Seeing Eye cat or bird? They will do all these things, and do them happily. Dogs will communicate with you by their facial expressions, tail movements, or vocally. What other pet can do this?

Vicky and the Fisherman

Some dogs can be a problem. When I was five, we had a boxer named Vicky. With me she was a beautiful, friendly loving dog. She loved to play, and would fetch a ball for hours. Unfortunately Vicky did not like grown men.

We got Vicky as a rescue dog at about age two, and I think she must have been abused by her previous owner. If a man came to our door Vicky would become mean. She would bark and snarl in a very threatening manner.

One day Dad took Vicky to the beach and she bit a fisherman so Dad had to leave her with a friend who had a nice farm. Dad never lied about anything, so of course this was the story my brothers and I all accepted.

Years later we somehow brought up the memory of Vicky to Dad and how she bit the fisherman. Dad scoffed, "I was the fisherman, and she bit _me_ in the butt!" "So you had to leave her at the farm right" we reminded him. "Farm HELL", Dad responded, "I took her to the Vet. The Vet asked if I wanted her put down, and I said no, I want you to KILL HER."

Dad was not one to mince words, but at least he was kind enough to save the real story for when we could better handle it.

A BOY HIS DOG AND A WELL

When I was young we lived on a farm. I had a dog, a Collie that might have been the smartest dog in the world. If you needed something from the workshop this dog would fetch it. "Go get a C-clamp". She would return with not just with a clamp, but a "C" clamp! One day while playing in the fields I fell into an abandoned well. I instructed my faithful friend "Go get Dad"...

"Joe"

Yes Dad.

"You never lived on a farm"

Are you sure?

"Positive, Timmy fell in the well. You are about to tell a story from "Lassie"."

Oh yeah, sorry. Never mind.

RT - Why do some people preface comments with expressions such as, "To tell you the truth…", "Honestly…", "The truth is…", "To be honest with you…", "Actually…etc. etc" Should I assume that without such an introduction they are not telling the truth?

COUNSELING

I wonder if anyone gets any help from counseling. My personal experience with marriage counseling is this is an outlet for the wife to complain about everything that ever happened in the relationship while some bespectacled geek sits and shakes his head at what a horrible person you are. The counselor always takes the wife's side, as the husband is incapable of actually expressing his feelings. The husband will not express his feelings as he has been conditioned to realize his feelings are wrong and invalid. They usually gets him in big trouble. This is probably the reason you are being counseled in the first place. The truth is, marriage counseling never solves a thing. It usually just makes the wife remember even more reasons why she is unhappy.

Counseling is the first step to the ultimate resolution, divorce. I have yet to meet a couple who went to counseling that did not end in divorce. Counseling is also used to punish the husband. When your spouse is pissed off at you, she will demand you see a counselor, knowing full well that a man would rather eat glass than sit with a stranger and discuss his feelings. After a session, your spouse has one more thing to bitch at you about. "You never said how you really felt, and if that was really how you feel, than you have a big problem, and you know I never do this and I always do that, and you never try to blah, blah, blah."

I think I could do this job.

"Welcome Mr. and Mrs. Smithers, Bob and Sally right? I'm Joe. I want you to know, what you say here stays here. Feel free to open up and say anything".

First let me make an observation. Bob, you need to lose about twenty pounds, you watch too much TV, especially football. You should help around the house more, earn more money, buy your wife flowers from time to time, walk the dog, take out the garbage, and pretty much treat Sally like a queen. Did I miss anything Sally? No? Well I guess we're all done then, with forty five minutes left. Any questions? OK then, Bob, shape up! That will be $130. Thank you, and I recommend the lawyer next door. He's very reasonable."

These days whenever anything bad happens in school they bring out about twenty "Grief Counselors" to make sure all the precious darlings can cope. "Children, Mary is out of class today with a severe hangnail. Anyone who is upset by this can go to the office and see a counselor". Is this my tax money hard at work?

When I was in school the announcement would be, "Children, Vinnie was hit by a bus this morning and was killed; now open your books to page 78. Does anyone know the answer to number 7?"

Child Counseling? Send the child to the waiting room and bring in the parents; they're the problem ninety percent of the time.

How does that make you feel?

RT - If perjury is a crime, why aren't all those who plead not guilty and are convicted also then convicted of perjury? Does this bother anyone else?

HIGH SCHOOL

High School years, I've been told, are the best years of your life. No wonder so many teens commit suicide. If as a teen I thought this was as good as life gets, I might have ended it all right there also. High School years are miserable. Acne, voice changing, raging hormones, trying to figure out girls, and trigonometry; what great fun!

High School is made up of four groups.

"The In Crowd"-This group walked about as if they owned the joint, preening, bragging and kissing the teachers asses as if their own shit did not stink. Those in the In Crowd were generally well to do, and enjoyed making fun of those who were not. "Attention KMART shopper" as they passed someone not dressed to their high hoity toity standards. Very funny you snobby stuck up vapid assholes! (If I was in the market the first time I heard this, I would have sold KMART short and been a rich man). I'm guessing this group was more miserable than they let on, always worried about what everyone thought, getting into the right College, driving the best car, and making friends with the wrong person which could get you thrown out of the In Crowd.

"The Misfits" - This group drank, smoked, got bad grades, and picked on anyone they thought they could get away with picking on. This was a group for whom High School made little sense. Some went on in life as successful trades people, entrepreneurs (drug dealers), or bums. Some went to Viet Nam and came back really screwed up. Others became firemen or cops and protected the same butts they used to kick. I liked the misfits better than the In Crowd.

"The Geeks" - The geeks were generally very smart, uncoordinated, immature, and oblivious to the fact that they were geeks. What happened to this group? With the development of computers and new technologies, the geeks did inherit the earth. Pity the poor In Crowder who ultimately ended up with a geek as their boss.

"The Tweeners"-I was a tweener, almost but not quite fitting in with the In Crowd, having several friends who were misfits, and respecting but keeping my distance from the geeks (it might be catching). Tweeners did whatever was necessary to get by and fly under the radar. When I was named captain of the football team, a first for someone not named Biff, I overheard an In Crowder express disbelief that Randy Burns was not named…… Randy was a pussey, you stuck up little shit!

I recently missed my ninth consecutive High School reunion. I was privy to an email with dozens of pictures of the glorious event. All were of the In Crowders, laughing and reliving the good old days. The email contents were full of the self-serving, high and mighty blather and crap that I remembered from those days of yore. Congratulations In Crowders; apparently those days **were** the best days of your lives.

I do have one small piece of information to help anyone get through this horrible institution. In English class, after every great novel, poem or play you study, you will be asked by your instructor, "What is the theme of this work. The dictionary defines this as: "a unifying or dominant idea, motif, etc., as in a work of art."

You will try to come up with something clever:

The theme to Melville's "Moby Dick" – Man's search to find the great white whale; or a more cerebral answer; a man's search to find his soul.

The theme to Twain's "Tom Sawyer" - A boy's journey into adulthood.

The theme to Poe's "The Raven" - A man's obsession with death.

No, no, and no.

The theme to every novel, poem or play you will ever study in high school is "Man's inhumanity to Man."

I know. It never made any sense to me either. I just do not believe Melville sat down to write "Moby Dick" thinking "This will really demonstrate Man's inhumanity to Man". Did Mark Twain think, "How can I show Man's inhumanity to Man"? Did Poe, in his cocaine addled mind wonder, "How can I best demonstrate Man's inhumanity to Man"? I don't think so either, but if you want a "very good" from your teacher, raise your hand and respond, "I believe the dominant idea the author was trying to convey was **Man's inhumanity to Man!**"

The theme to this work is that man is all screwed up, but if anyone asks, just say Mr. Hagy is clearly conveying Man's inhumanity to Man. Just trust me on this one.

One more word of advice to any young lad currently in High School; treat all the girls nicely! You see that chubby one with zits and bad teeth? In five years she just might be the hottest girl in town. It happens all the time. The hottie you're chasing after could be living in a trailer park with three kids in five years.

RT - I don't know how women won the toilet seat battle. Their argument of falling into the bowl in the middle of the night just does not hold any water (excuse the expression). Just put the damn seat down, problem over. How would they like it if I forgot to put the seat up in the middle of the night? Sit down in that if you are looking for an unpleasant two AM surprise! Men, don't fight this rule. It's over, put it down when you're done....

I'm just saying.

CONCERTS

My new girlfriend loves concerts. I hate them. I recently began going to concerts.

At sixty bucks a seat, I expect to be entertained; I refuse to clap rhythmically because the headliner tells me to. I hate the back and forth arm waving that if Mr. Bigshot Star does not get he stops the act. Please keep me out of your act. I'm not going to pick a card, hold a hat or get in a box for your magic act. You need an assistant, give me a discount! Listen, Mr. Comedian, if I wanted some asshole to poke fun at me for other's amusement I'd go back to High School!

Members of the audience at these functions also annoy me. Why do I always get behind the loud high clapper? These attention seeking super fans will do anything to have the star notice them. Arms extended so everyone can see them clap, they are always the last to stop applauding. Sometimes you have a high clapper on either side of the theater, and it becomes a gotcha last contest. Can we just get on with the show? The singer starts a song that everyone in the room knows, and the super fans have to yell and scream. We get it; you know the song!

Then there is the mandatory "We love you Johnny" cry from some idiot waiting for the "I love you too" reply. Speak for yourself; maybe I only **like** Johnny! We went to a Cindy Lauper concert and these idiots started the "We love you Cindy" call. Cindy stopped her song and replied in her cartoon voice, "You don't even know me, and how do you love me? I might be a real shit for all you know." "Love the performance, not the performer", she said. Now **I** love Cindy Lauper!

Some fool always has to shout out a song for the performer to sing. Give it some time Dude; I'm pretty sure Cindy just might eventually get around to singing "Girls Just Want To Have Fun!"

If the joke or story is funny, laugh. There is no need to applaud in order to show you get it. Gay people are especially guilty of this crap. Any joke with a gay reference is greeted with thunderous applause. "Look at me, I'm gay, I get it." I have nothing against gay people, but why are they so insistent to revel in their gayness at concerts? Some are almost angry about it. It's like "Hey that's right, I'm gay. What are you going to do about it?" NOTHING, we don't care! "I'm heterosexual. Want to make something about it?"

It's really embarrassing when the super fan stands up and high claps and no one else follows. How long should he stand and applaud by himself? This must really be a slap in the face for the performer.

This is my favorite part of any concert.

SMOKING

That's right, I am a smoker. I don't smoke pot; that would be cool. I don't smoke crack; that would invoke pity. I smoke tobacco. I am not proud of this fact, but with my fellow smokers, at least we provide a group that it is politically correct to hate.

I have to endure face to face comments from strangers, in open spaces, "Oooh, a smoker!" Does anyone go up to a fat person and say, "Oooh, a glutton!"? People walk up to me and ask, "Do you know that's not good for you?" "Really", Is that why every pack has a message from the surgeon general saying "THIS SHIT CAN KILL YOU"? Does anyone walk up to an obese person and say, "Do you know that eating like a fucking pig can kill you"? NO! But it is ok to say that crap to a smoker. We pay tons of money in taxes for our habit; shouldn't fat people pay a tax on the extra calories they consume?

Sorry again for the language Tommy, Halley, Graham, Cole and Connor; Grandpa Joe gets a little testy about this subject. (I had to mention my Grand Children or I'd be in big trouble.)

We are accused of killing others with second hand smoke, and driving up health care prices with smoking related diseases. The second hand smoke claim is probably crap, and if true, current laws and common courtesy demands I only smoke outside. I am OK with that. The health care claim is ridiculous. It assumes without smoking I would never get ill and take up medical resources. We all get sick, take up medical resources and die. Smokers just tend to go through this cycle earlier. You could make the argument that we die earlier and quicker, taking up less resources. You don't see smokers languishing in nursing homes at age 95.

I know, I know, Smoking is not good. It is very bad, and I should quit. I have quit several times, and will probably quit again, but it is not easy. If you want someone to quit, leave them alone. Nagging is not an inducement to quit. How about a little sympathy for our affliction, or does it just make people feel better about themselves to have a group to hate?

And please, for God sake, keep your precocious little four year olds away. "Do you know that's bad for you?" Out of the mouths of babes. YES, I friggin know! Come back and talk to me in 15 years and let's see how great your life is. I'm not listening to someone who might be a future crack whore!

Never mind how I became addicted. Yes smoking is an addiction, not a habit, and it is very hard to not light up. How hard is it? Have you ever had a scab on your elbow and tried not to pick it? Have you ever been on a diet and had to say no to a jelly donut? Have you ever been cut off on the highway and stopped from flipping the guy the bird? Have you ever had a mosquito bite and been told not to scratch it? Has someone ever farted in church, and you tried not to laugh? Has someone ever pissed you off, and it just wasn't the time or place to not bite your lip and shut up? Have you ever had to pee, and the next rest stop is fifteen miles away? Have you ever been really horny and tried not to touch yourself?

It is not easy!

I'm sorry, but when I see some power walking, plastic bottle of Poland Spring water drinking (I think I read somewhere that drinking from plastic bottles was not good for you), non smoking, no alcohol drinking, no red meat eating, special walking shoes and helmet with rear view mirror wearing, uptight know it all, I think the extra five years of living he thinks he is getting just went down the drain.

OK, it's just me.

RT - My favorite Girl Scout cookie was the "Samoa". Then this delicious treat was renamed "Caramel Delight". Did the name of a cookie upset Samoans? Are we that crazy politically correct? You can name a cookie Whitey, Honkey, WASP, The Joe, or The Nerdy European White Bread Smuck and I would not be offended. Apparently the Girl Scouts were concerned an entire island would boycott their cookie even though they had been sold with the same name for as long as I can remember.

Guess what? This year they're named Samoas again. Probably some 350 pound islander stomped into GS headquarters and demanded "Where's my COOKIE?"

PORNOGRAPHY

I have never bought, read, or even heard of Playboy, Hustler, Penthouse, Boobs, Beaver Patrol or Jugs magazines. I have never heard of performers such as Jenna Jameson, Misty Stone, Randy Spears, Katie Kox, Amber Rayne, Aaron Wilcoxxx, Meggan Mallone, John Holmes, or Belladonna. I have never seen movies called Porno Workout, 30 Love, Girlvert, or Squirt. I would not even know how to find internet sites such as Asian Fever, Big Butt Hos, Roxy Reynolds XXX, or AVN. I would never enter one of those sleazy Adult Stores with their nasty movies, lotions, toys, and private booths, and I would never even approach the nasty looking clerk behind the window three feet above the main floor.

Clearly I am unqualified to have an opinion on this subject! But for sure, anything involving chickens and not Colonel Sanders is pornography.

WAR

If there is one area where God must second guess his decision to give us mortals free will, it would be war.

"Jesus Christ, what was I thinking?"

"Excuse me?"

"Not you Jesus. It's just an expression."

"Oh God!"

"Yes"

"Not you God. It was just an expression."

"Jesus Christ, cut that out" "Jesus"… "Jesus I'm talking to you!"

"What?"

"Never mind"

"Oh God!"

"Yes"

"Never mind"

"Holy Mother of God!"

"What?"

"Not you Mary. I'm just talking out loud."

"Jesus!"

"What Mom?"

"Everyone just STOP IT! Do you see what those idiots are doing down there? Now they're about to blow up everything and all over you and Mohammed!"

"What?"

"Never mind Mohammed; *Jesus, Mary and Joseph.*"

"What?"

"What?"

"What?"

"NEVER MIND!"

Almost all Wars have been fought through the years over land, resources, or how to worship God. I'm pretty sure God doesn't care how we worship and would rather we just choose our own way and leave others alone. However, he gave us free will and this is how we often choose to use it.

Fighting over land is also stupid as there is so much of it; unfortunately there are people who just want it all. The Jews didn't fight for land for years and ended being pushed around and hated by everyone else. Enough is enough. They now have the only hunk of desert in the Middle East without any oil and they still have to fight for that!

There are no good wars, but some just have to be fought. Generally those who start a war never actually have to fight in it. If they did, I think there would not be any wars. There should be a rule: you start it, and you go to the front line. I'll wager world Leaders would become very good at compromising.

During the so called "Cold War" between the USSR and the United States both sides spent huge percentages of their economic output on preparing for war and or defense. At dinner one night, Dad expressed how ridiculous this was. "What we ought to do", he said, "Is spend all that money on millions of cars, washers and dryers, dishwashers and such. Load them all on ships and deliver them all to Russia. The Russians would then have to use all their resources building roads and electric plants and grids. No one would have the time or money to start a war!"

"Jesus, that's what they should be doing!"

"What?"

"Never mind Jesus; I was just thinking out loud again."

I cannot even imagine how horrible it must be to have to fight in one of these wars. The hardships and lost lives of those who endured conflict to save and protect their fellow citizens from those who just want it all should never be forgotten. These brave men (ok and women) cannot be thanked enough. I believe, for starters, that any service person who was stationed in a combat zone should be exempt from taxes. They paid enough! Further, if you see a man in uniform, just stop and tell him thanks. If you see a man in uniform at a bar or restaurant, his money should be no good; step up and cover his bill. It is the right thing to do. The biggest disgrace of the Viet Nam war was not just that we fought it, but that our soldiers (most all of whom were drafted) were received back home to jeers, not cheers.

As horrible as wars are today, how did soldiers of yesteryear even follow orders?

"OK men. I want you all to line up in several rows. We are going to march out to that open field toward their rows of men and when I give the signal start firing. There are more of us than them so we are bound to win."

"Are you crazy General?"

"Or we can just hang you right here!"

"Ah....this line?"

In the middle ages wars were extra brutal.

"Men, we have been chosen for a very important duty. Jonesy take your guys and bring your ladders. Your job is to race through the hail storm of arrows, reach the castle, and take on the barrels of boiling oil they will drop on you. Then the rest of us will hoist the ladders and storm the castle. Got it?"

"Umm"

"Or we could just hang you right here"... "Jonesy?"

"I'm thinking, I'm thinking!"

Instead of wars, why can't we just settle things with a contest? You want to take on the United States? We choose football. You want a piece of Brazil? Better get your soccer team prepared. Take on India? I hope you can spell. Don't even try to mess around in Asia if you can't do the math.

I'm just saying, for God sake!

"What?"

Never mind.

RT - Pigeons must be the stupidest creatures on Earth. Have you ever watched them eat a piece of bread? Every one of them grabs the bread with their beak and shakes it until the piece is thrown away about six feet and they are left with a tiny crumb to devourer. Each time they grab the piece of bread, they miss stepping on it by about one sixteenth of an inch. You would think that in all the years of feeding pigeons bread, just one time one of these stupid birds would accidentally step on the damn bread. All the other pigeons would then realize "wow that's a good idea, hold the bread down with a claw, and we can eat to our hearts content!"

You can take these same birds blindfolded 500 miles from their coop, let them go, and they will find their way home. Go figure. Do you not think that God has a sense of humor?

"Moses, Mohammed, Jesus, Mary and Joseph; come over here. Check out the Pigeons. They still won't step on the bread. I tell you that is almost as funny as the giraffe I created."

NAMES

No one names their children Bob, Bill, Jane or Mary anymore. White people are now all named Cody, Ashley, Brent, Tyler, Cole, Halley, Graham, Spencer, Connor (ok I'm guilty too) or Todd. I guess we think our kids will have original names. What a surprise when they get to first grade and eight kids named Todd all raise their hands.

The Irish all name their boys Sean, Brian, or Mike. Their girl's names must end with een: Kathleen, Irene, Eileen, Helene, Aileen, Doreen, Josephine, Gasoline ... If it ends with an een it is Irish.

Black people all have unique names. Their names are like snowflakes; no two are alike. (I can't prove it, but the other day it snowed and I swear I saw two flakes that were identical.) I think Black children are named with a Boggle cup. They shake it up, roll out the letters and have 15 seconds to come up with a name. Why is that racist? Come on; Oprah, Anfreney, Lashon, La shonda, Noshon, La Bron, Shaquille, and Kobe? I understand why names such as Amos, Tom, Jemima, or Andy are out; I'm just saying. And what is with all the Sha's and La's? For some reason Blacks never use the letter "C", only "K" or "Qu".

The country passed laws against asking about race on applications for anything such as jobs, school or loans to limit prejudice in the selection process. If your application IS processed by a racist, the name KaSheequa just might be to your disadvantage.

Celebrities have to give their children names like Apple, Flower, Peace, Blanket, Chastity or Petal. What up wid dat? I could understand Oscar or Emmy, but Blanket?

I went to an Indian Restaurant the other night and there was a big fight. I don't know what happened. We were waiting for a table with about 35 other people when the announcement was made "Patel, table for four". Next thing I knew, all Hell broke loose!

I wish we could at least agree how to spell names. Sean becomes Chon, or Shon. It's crazy. Why would parents make their children go through life having to explain "that's Bill with one L all the time?" or "No that's jhonny, not Johnny." Some people even get angry about the spelling, "THAT'S Katie with an "I", K-A-T-I." Drives me knuts!

"I have a pet dogg. No, it's dog with two g's, and I also have a pet Kat!

When I was five years old, everyone called me Jody (that's Jody with a Y). When I saw the movie "Old Yeller" there was a girl in it named Jody. I freaked out, and have been Joe ever since.

My cousin Neils still calls me Jody. He never met me as Jody and probably heard me referred to as Jody about five times 58 years ago and he still says, "I just can't get used to calling you Joe!" In the mean time, he has gone from Neils to Nelson, to Neil, to Nels, to Niles and to Nils. If you get HIS name wrong he gets angry about it!

I do like Neils, Nelson, Neil, Nels, Niles, Nils, but sometimes he can be casual about things in a funny way. About twenty years ago we had a family reunion. I had not seen Neils, Nelson, Neil, Nels, Niles, Nils for at least ten years and didn't have much to talk to him about. Another cousin told me that Neils, Nelson, Neil, Nels, Niles, Nils had a hobby raising chicken hawks. Apparently there was a story in the paper about his hobby. He was raising 50 chicken hawks in his garage! Fascinating, I thought. When I went up to Neils, Nelson, Neil, Nels, Niles, Nils, I said, "So Niles, I hear you have a hobby raising hawks."

"That's NILS!"

"So Nils, I hear you have a hobby raising hawks."

"Yeah, so?"

I thought if raising 50 chicken hawks in your garage is not interesting, what the hell else is he up to?

American Indians give names based on the individual's characteristics. Running Bear, Sitting Bull, Dances With Wolves, Walks On Light Feet and so on. Mobsters do the same: Tony The Gimp, Vito Big Nose, Vinnie Bag Of Donuts.

Whatever! As Shakespeare said, "What is in a name?"

RT - How do blind people know when they are done wiping?

"OH MILTON!"

"What? He's your grandson."

"Well he did not get that stuff from me!"

Sorry Grandma, Sorry Grandpa.

"It is a good question though."

"MILTON!!"

MICKEY MANTLE and FREDDY DERODA

1956 was a magical year for Yankee fans. The Yankees won the pennant, and recaptured the World Series title which they had given up to the hated Dodgers the year before. Don Larson threw the only World Series perfect game, and Mickey Mantle hit the homerun which assured that victory. 1956 was the year Mickey won the triple crown, leading the league with 52 homeruns, 130 RBIs and a batting average of .353. Mickey was every 10 year old's idol.

In the summer of 1957, Mickey Mantle was coming to Manhasset, Long Island to sell and sign his new book, "The Mickey Mantle Story".

This review is from: The Mickey Mantle Story, (Hardcover)

The childhood story of Mickey Mantle's father pitching to him first as he hit from the right side, and then from the left is the beginning of the story of a baseball legend. Mantle was considered by many to be the greatest natural athlete who ever played the game. He was probably the greatest switch-hitter of all times, and his career mark of five hundred and thirty six homers is still impressive. He played on the great Yankee teams in which there also played his buddy Whitey Ford, and also Maris, Yogi Berra, and Billy Martin. Mantle was injury-prone and this hurt his career. But the really tragic part of his story is the genetic disease which haunted him throughout his life. In terms of power and speed when he was at his best, there was no one like him.

The "Mick" was coming to town! I saved for weeks and raided my milk bottle of change to scrape up the $7.00 price of this life story of the most famous 25 year old in New York. When the day came I stood with Mom in a line fifty yards away from the bookstore entrance. Mickey was scheduled to sign for two hours. After an hour, the line had moved only ten yards. I left Mom to see what was holding things up and found the entrance jammed with an unorganized scramble of line cutters. The only way in was to also cut the line. Mom of course said no. Cutting was wrong, and you should not stoop to other's transgressions.

For one time in my brief life I did not listen to Mom. I left and went to the front, ducked, dodged dipped and crawled to the entrance and reached the real line to see "The Mick." Ten minutes before he was scheduled to leave I was in front of my idol. It was the first time I had ever stood face to face with a real celebrity.

The Mick was great; he took my $7.00 and asked with his Mickey Mantle smile and Oklahoma charm, "How do you want me to sign it kid?" "Joe" I managed to blurt out, "To Joe." And so I went home as probably the only eleven year old in Manhasset with an autographed copy of "The Mickey Mantle Story", "To Joe, best wishes Mickey Mantle."

This became my favorite possession-a puff piece slapped together to capitalize on Mickey's Triple Crown year, autographed to ME! "The Mickey Mantle Story" somehow left out the accounts of Mickey's boozing and womanizing that became legendary years later, but it would not have mattered to me.

At night, listening to the game on WINS radio, I would hold "The Book" as I listened. When Mickey came to bat, in a crucial situation, I would rub "The Autograph", and almost as often as not Mickey would deliver a homerun. I, of course, took some credit; rubbing the autograph and a homerun could not have been a coincidence. There was a bond between the Mick and me even if he did not know it. The Mick was from Oklahoma; I was born in Oklahoma and called it home the first eight months of my life, so "the Book", "The Autograph" and I held a special power.

I was the envy of the neighborhood because of my prized possession-especially to FREDDY DERODA.

Freddy lived about two blocks away. He was a rich kid who lived in the only custom built home in the Munsey Park section of Manhasset. Freddy was only a casual friend, though he and his Father did once take me bowling. Even Dad was impressed when they picked me up in their Bentley, and Dad was not easily impressed by material possessions.

Winter vacation 1959, Freddy asked to "borrow" "The Book" which he needed for a book report. I reluctantly lent him "The Book". How could you not trust a kid whose father drove a Bentley? When I returned to school after

Christmas, Freddy was absent. He was absent the next three days. I rode to his house to see if Freddy was alright (and to get my book back).

His house was empty - no furniture, no Bentley, no Freddy, NO BOOK! The Derodas had moved. Quickly and quietly they had moved in the middle of the night. No one knew where or why. Freddy had known, but told no one, and he used the opportunity to escape with my book.

I pedaled home in shock. Theft did not happen in Manhasset. We did not lock up our bikes, you could leave your car running if you were going to make a quick stop in the store, and homes were left unlocked all day. Yet, my BOOK was stolen! It was stolen by FREDDY DERODA.

To this day the name affects me. FREDDY DERODA. "Slowly I turn, step by step, inch by inch". It makes me want to break or KILL something.

Mickey still had some good years, especially 1961, but he was slowed by debilitating injuries and as great as he was, he never really reached his full potential for greatness. I think it had something to do with "The Book", "The Autograph", and our now broken "special connection".

Reflecting today, I have a feeling that Mr. Deroda might have been a member of that special Union which did not allow striking, or leaving, and the Derodas had no choice but to leave on the sly, in the dead of night. This must have been devastating to an eleven year old boy. That he could leave with one special thing of value must have been important to him. Freddy, I hope "The Book" helped you through what must have been a hard time; I guess I forgive you.

THE COIN COLLECTION
(guest reminiscence from Chris)

I sent Chris an email with the Freddy Deroda story and he returned this story:

Deroda is like Bob Houseman. Do you remember him? He lived on Waverly Road, in San Marino Ca., across the street and up a house or two from us. He was a bit of a geek, a year younger than Jim, who would have nothing to do with him because of his high geek rating, but he was a year older than me and I played with him from time to time. It must have been 1952 or '53 (because I think we moved to Robles Road in late '53 or early '54 and then to Manhasset in '55). He and I were in the back in the room which we shared (and awoke every morning to "I got all the space men"). I was letting him look through the coin collection.

This was a collection which Grandpa had given to Jim and me (possibly before you were born) Grandpa's collection was (still is) pretty extensive with almost every penny, nickel, and dime from 1890-1952. The prides of the collection were some "Barber" Quarters which dated back to 1892. They were beautiful things in near mint condition.

While we were playing, Mom called me to lunch. I left Bob Houseman in our room as he was still looking at the collection, and I expected we would still hang out after lunch. During lunch I recall him yelling "see you later" and he was quickly out the door. Not long after, while putting "The Collection" away I realized that not only was Houseman gone, but about $8 in face value of the beautiful quarters were also absent. These quarters were probably actually worth closer to $150 to collectors, and even then were not that easy to replace.

I ran to his house but no one was home. His family had left for a vacation in the mountains. The dumb SOB took Grandpa's quarters with him and spent them on $8.00 worth of comic books and candy.

Unlike Freddy Deroda, Bob Houseman had to come home. When he did Jim finally took a definite interest in the geek. Jim beat a confession out of Bob Houseman. There were no Miranda warnings required at the time so we deemed his bloodied confession to be voluntary and told his folks.

They did pay us something–maybe $50, and I remember going up to some coin store on Colorado Blvd. in Pasadena to replace the Barber quarters. I was not able to replace all the quarters and somehow those store-bought quarters were just not as beautiful as the ones which Grandpa had given us.

Speaking of the coin collection I still feel guilty about this little nerdy kid in school whom I had befriended because he also liked to collect coins and we sometimes would trade. He had these bottle thick glasses and even with the magnifying glass he didn't see very well. I traded him a mercury headed dime for a 1909 Indian head penny. Or so he thought.

I could make out that it was a 1909-s which was pretty rare. It was worth about $10 even in those days, and it is now one of the most valuable coins in the collection. It is also the coin I have the most guilt about. The idea of coin trading among friends should not be to try and trade something of lesser value for something of greater value, especially without full disclosure. I never told the kid. Fact is, until now I don't believe I have told anyone about my "outfoxing" the blind kid. (See Joe, the Garbageboatwalk deal wasn't my first steal.)

"I Got All The Space Men"

Well Chris mentioned it, so now I've got to tell it. I was only five so I am a little fuzzy on the details. Any resemblance to this story and Bill Cosby's "Turtle Heads" story is strictly a case of brothers all over being about the same.

In 1951 we moved from Roslyn, L.I. to San Marino, California. We lived in a three bedroom ranch house. It really had four bedrooms if you count a large closet with a window which was stuffed full with boxes from the cross country move. Jim was the oldest so he got his own room. Chris and I shared the other; for about a week.

When we woke up the very first morning, Chris asked me to do something of which I do not remember. I asked him why me and he said "Because I'm bigger." Where the next response came from I also do not remember, but it went something like this:

"Oh yeah, well I got all the soldiers!"

"It won't do you any good, because I got all the guns."

The next morning I was up first, and woke Chris with:

"I got all the soldiers, and I got all the guns!"

"It won't do you any good, because I got all the planes and bombs."

The next morning I was up first and woke Chris with:

"I got all the soldiers, all the guns, and I got all the planes and bombs!"

"It won't do you any good, because I got all the ray guns, and they can blast all your planes."

"MOM!!!"

"Jim, Chris, Joe, What's going on its just 6:30 in the morning"

"Chris has all the ray guns and he's going to blast my planes."

"Oh for goodness sakes ignore him!....Hells Bells!"

Mom's advice to Chris' torments was always to ignore it; "Hells Bells" meant she was getting upset. Had she said "Dammit-to-Hell", we would have both been scared.

The next morning I was up first and woke Chris with:

"I got all the soldiers, all the guns, all the planes and bombs, and all the ray guns!"

"Won't do you any good, because I got all the space men, and they control the ray guns because only they know how to use them, you can't have the ray guns without the space men"

"MOM!!!"

"Jim, Chris, Joe, it's 6:00 in the morning!"

"Chris has all the space men and only they know how to use the ray guns so they control them."

"Oh for heaven sake, just cut it out, I'm tired of this nonsense."

The next morning I woke up screaming, "I got all the soldiers, the guns, the planes and bombs, the ray guns, and I GOT ALL THE SPACE MEN!"

It won't do you any good, Chris snarled, "BECAUSE I'M STILL BIGGER!"

"MOM!!!"

Dammit-to-Hell!!

That night the closet with a window was cleared, and we all had our own rooms.

TECHNOLOGY

There is always a price to pay for progress.

"You can have a telephone, but you lose your privacy and the charm of distance. You can conquer the skies, but the birds will lose their wonder and the clouds will smell of gasoline" (Spencer Tracy in "Inherit The Wind").

"You can have 260 channels, but you lose the intimacy and charm of easy selection; and your eyes will blur from flipping." (Joe Hagy).

The world saw almost no technology changes after the first invention of primitive tools. Until the middle of the nineteenth century things stayed pretty much the same. Then we had the industrial age, communication age, the computer age, and the information highway. There have been more changes in the way we live our lives in the last one hundred and twenty five years, than in the previous two thousand years.

Most of these changes have been pure improvements; car safety improvements have only been positive, GPS systems have brought nothing but reduced tension in travel, improved health care is only a plus, and who could ever go back to one-ply toilet paper?

Some technology changes have, however, come at a price particularly to us older farts.

(I don't really consider myself as old yet. When I am introduced at a birthday as being xx years YOUNG, I will know I am really OLD.)

As a teen, we had one black rotary telephone. AT+T owned the phone, and every extra phone was an additional charge every month. Anything except black cost extra, and a touch tone was an extravagance we could live without. Calling a girl for a date generally took three hang-ups before I could actually muster the courage to ask to speak to Susie. If we had caller ID in those days, I would have been dateless until I reached college.

I hate call-waiting; I have enough trouble focusing on one person at a time. Star 69? I once hung up the phone before it was answered when I realized I had dialed the wrong number. This lady star 69nd me to tell me how rude I was. "Ahhm towwy laadee". If Spencer Tracy thought the telephone stole your privacy and the charm of distance, he should have stayed around for the cell phone, and text messaging!

I hate IPODs. How much music can a person listen to? I don't even know 2000 songs, never mind down loading them to a device. Spencer and I were walking on the beach one summer and we spotted a pod of dolphins circling bait fish about 100 yards off shore. They trapped these fish in a ring and took turns leaping through the middle feasting on their trapped prey. It was a National Geographic "Big Blue Marble" moment. Three groups of joggers passed with their IPODs plugged in and they missed it all. Without the IPODs, we were able to appreciate the really cool dolphin POD.

I do admit I love cable TV and TVOING. I don't think I could live without the remote. When we were young, Jim and Chris had the original remote - ME.

"Joe, change the channel."

"Why"

" 'Cause I said so"

I flipped from "King Kong" to "Charlie Chan" to Basketball, and back to "King Kong". I never left the knob. If we had 260 channels I would have permanent Carpal Tunnel Syndrome.

The computer and the internet are great, but they interfere with my TV time. Emails are dangerous. If you are not careful emails are easily misinterpreted. That funny thing you think you said loses something on the other end and can get you in trouble. I try to use emails for communicating information only. Casual use on emails in business has put many a transgressor in jail.

My son loves the Wii and XBOX, but he will never know the interaction and fun of board-games, knock hockey and electric football. It took 20 minutes to set up a play in electric football, but when "Jim Brown" broke one through the middle for a TD, it was the best! (Does anyone else remember boiling the rubber feet and then having to figure out which ones would run straight, and which ones you would use for your end around?)

I would comment on Twittering and Blogging, but I still don't know what the heck they are.

Like it or not, you cannot turn back from technological improvements. I'm sure there were old timers who preferred the Ox and plow to a John Deere; so I know it's just me.

RT - How to impress the boss:

Do you want to climb the corporate ladder? You had better learn corporate speak. Here is an example:

Well sir, from our **client's perspective** the **accessibility of data necessitates** a **user friendly platform** which will **provide added value**. We need to **get on the same page**.

From an IT **perspective**, we need to **think outside the box** and develop a more **interactive, seamless** and **robust environment**, which, **going forward**, will **positively influence** the firm's **bottom line**. Having said that, **the fact of the matter is** our competitor's systems upgrade has put us at an **increased disadvantage** which **at the end of the day** will **negatively impact** the financial **goals** of the firm.

Words such as perspective, interactive, seamless and robust cannot be used enough. Robust is an absolutely required word in any discussion. Never say improve when you can say positively influence. Never say reduce when you can say negatively impact. Any dissertation must include the phrases: user friendly, having said that, on the same page, think outside the box, added value, going forward, bottom line, the fact of the matter, and at the end of the day.

"Our customers are moving to the other guys because their stuff works better than our stuff and we need to improve fast or we will be out of business", is one reason I am retired.

But, what do I know?

CELEBRITIES

In general, I am not fond of celebrities. I guess if you are constantly receiving awards, there are always people around to serve your every need, and your ass is kissed every day you begin to catch a bit of an attitude.

Celebrity athletes aren't too bad. At least their failures are acknowledged and this brings them back to earth a little bit. The worst are actors, singers and supermodels.

Actors have about 25 different award shows to constantly remind them how special they are; Oscar, Emmy, The Golden Globe, Cannes Film fest, American Comedy Award, Saturn Award, Blockbuster Entertainer Award, Golden Apple Award, Hollywood Film Festival, MTV Awards, People's Choice Award, Screen Actor's Guild, TV Land Award, and Film Critics' Awards from virtually every city in the world to name a few. What do you call an actor without an award? Waiter.

Singers receive a few awards as well; here is a list of awards given to Beyonce:

2.1 American Music Awards
2.2 American Society of Composers, Authors, and Publishers (ASCAP), USA
2.3 BET Awards, USA
2.4 Billboard Music Magazine, USA
2.5 BRAVO Supershow, Germany
2.6 BRIT Awards, UK
2.7 Capital FM Awards, UK
2.8 Demand International Entertainer of The Year
2.9 Glamour Magazine Woman of the Year, UK
2.10 Grammy Awards, USA

2.11 International Dance Music Awards, World
2.12 Ivor Novello Awards
2.13 Latin Grammy Awards
2.14 Meteor Music Awards, Ireland
2.15 Music of Black Origin Awards, UK (MOBO)
2.16 Music Television, World (MTV)
2.17 NAACP Image Awards
2.18 New Musical Express, UK (NME)
2.19 Nickelodeon Kids' Choice Awards
2.20 NRJ Music Awards (France)
2.21 People Choice Awards, USA
2.23 Premios Fuse TV
2.24 Premios Lo Nuestro
2.25 Premios Oye, Mexico
2.26 Radio Music Awards, USA
2.27 Soul Train Music Awards, USA
2.28 Source Hip-Hop Music Awards, USA
2.29 Teen Choice Awards
2.30 The Record of the Year, UK (ITV)
2.31 Urban Music Awards
2.32 VH1, USA
2.33 Vibe Awards, USA
2.34 Whudat Music Awards, USA
2.35 World Music Awards, World

Do you think she feels "Special"?

Supermodels may not have as many awards, but I'm guessing that seeing yourself on ten different magazine covers a month might give you a bit of an ego.

I love it when one of these prima donnas is interviewed.

"So Bobbie Jo, is modeling really as glamorous as it looks?"

"You know Jay, that is what people think, but I have to get up at five AM for a shoot. In the chair for hair and makeup at five thirty, on the set at seven, then you sit around for hours as they adjust the lighting and stuff, then pose, and sit while they make more adjustments, pose and sit, pose and sit, sometimes until ten PM."   All for only $50,000!

Have you ever watched "The Deadliest Catch"? These guys go out on the treacherous Bering Sea in the dead of winter, minus 20 wind chill, and work their asses off twenty hours a day for three weeks straight trying to catch crab. If they are lucky and don't get killed and they catch a lot of crab, they might walk away with $50,000. I don't know about you, but I would rather pose and sit and pose and sit.

What if: What if these lucky bastards were born in 1850? No models to speak of, and actors and singers were considered the low life of society.

I enjoy a good play, movie, TV show, CD or a concert, but do I have to hear these people's opinions on everything: politics, health care, global warming, world peace, economics......oh yeah, that's what I'm doing. But no one is listening to me!

I remember one actor was asked his opinion on some deep subject (I think it was Dinero) and he answered, "What the hell are you asking me for? All I do is pretend to be someone else for a living." Good answer.

Since I have never actually met a celebrity (except 15 seconds with "The Mick") I guess I hate them all. There a few I think I would like:

Robert Dinero - I'm assuming it was he who made the above comment.

Tom Hanks - He just seems like a down to earth guy on the talk shows, and I heard he is good friends with his chauffer.

Derek Jeter - You gotta like the Yankee Captain.

~~Tiger Woods - He has that nice smile, is a great golfer, and is a great family man.~~

Chris Rock - Too funny not to like!

Merl Streep - Super talented and seems grounded on talk shows. She is also from New Jersey.

Howard Stern - Probably a bastard to work for, but loyal to those that can put up with him. Plus he spends four hours a day, four days a week entertaining with his random thoughts opinions and reminiscences. I have no idea how he does it!

There must be others, but off hand I can't think of any.

RT - Did you know that? Did you know that people who have half moons under their fingernails are part African?

Did you look?

RT - If man is so smart, why can't someone invent popcorn without the kernels that stick in your teeth?

POLITICS

Our political system is probably the most inefficient system in the world. Passing any legislation requires a passing vote in the house, a passing vote in the Senate, which usually goes back to the house to vote on the changed version, back to the Senate and finally has to be signed by the President. After this lengthy process the legislation can still be subject to being overturned by the Supreme Court. The beauty of our political system is that it is very inefficient.

The most efficient political systems are those run by a dictator, or Monarch. New laws and rules under those systems are created instantaneously at the whim of the Leader. This is terrific if your ruler is benevolent and really smart. This is almost never the case. A benevolent dictator by his very nature is probably not capable of holding his power over those who would take it from him.

Hitler got things done very fast. I very much doubt that the power to kill nine million people could ever be pushed through two legislative branches, get signed by a President all of whom are subject to being voted out of power. If it were possible I suspect the Supreme Court might find extermination of a race or religious group to be against our Constitution.

So while we complain of Washington's inability to get things done, we should also rejoice in this very same inability. In an emergency, when push comes to shove, our politicians manage to act together and act quickly.

Otherwise most political decisions are part of a big game; the winner of the game gets reelected. That our political system is a game sounds horrible, but it is this "game" which ultimately results in rule by the majority of our citizens. There are of course times when the majority of our citizens are terribly wrong, but when mistakes become obvious, they are usually corrected. It takes time, but the system seems to work.

We could make some changes to allow our system to work more efficiently and still maintain the balance of power, and rule by the people which are the foundations of our political process. To make this happen I am willing to be appointed temporary benevolent dictator.

As temporary benevolent dictator I decree the following:

Term limits for congressmen are now two terms of two years.

Term limits for Senators are now two terms of four years.

The President will continue to limit his time in office to two four year terms.

Our legislators should hold office at a sacrifice and act as servants of the people. The founders of the Constitution never envisioned professional politicians, but instead expected leaders who would consider such service to be an honor. Term limits will reduce the incentive for people to seek power for power's sake.

The President has the power of a line item veto. Legislation presented to the President for his signature must be related. He will not be forced to sign a health care bill which also grants money to Minnesota to build a 100 million dollar speed skating facility.

The Supreme Court is hereby abolished. All laws requiring judicial review will be presented to Judge Judy.

Have you ever seen Judge Judy on TV? Judge Judy will streamline the judicial process. Faced with thousands of pages of testimony and arguments why we should or should not allow burning of the Flag, unlimited and unrestricted abortion on demand, Christmas Trees on public property, Gay Marriage or other such cases she would simply say, "Do I look like an idiot! Don't come here with your cockamamie arguments. You just can't do this and you can't do that because it does not make sense and if it doesn't make sense it can't be true. Next case. Come on I'm not getting any younger. Bert, throw that Harvard Law clown out of here. It's almost lunch time. NEXT CASE!"

Lawyers will be fined for frivolous law suits. A judge will decide this before the defendant has to spend millions to defend nonsense. I once received a check for 15 cents as part of a class action suit against Chrysler. Apparently they left out a comma in their lease contract which made the agreement confusing. Confusing? No one can read all those pages of fine print in the first place. The sales guy explains what it says. You look at the numbers and you sign. Chrysler probably spent $1,000,000 dollars to settle this case for $200,000. I got 15 cents and some schlock lawyer gets a $75,000 fee for finding the missing comma. We can do better than that.

From this day forth, in order to make Atheists happy, all government references to "In God We Trust" will read "In God We Trust... or not." The Pledge Of Allegiance will read "One Nation under God; maybe."

Income tax is now abolished. There will be government agents empowered to randomly stop any one and demand all his money. The person stopped will be given a card exempting him from being stopped again for six weeks. Robbery is robbery.

There will be a 10% tax on the sale of anything that says Aviation or Marine; if you are buying such a product, you must be rich.

If you look both ways and see no approaching cars you may cross against a red light.

It is OK to yell "fire" in a crowded movie theater, if there actually is a fire.

It is not OK to yell "get in the hole" at golf tournaments even if it looks like the ball will actually get in the hole.

The death penalty is now abolished. However if you are convicted of a capital crime, prison guards will be allowed to give you a wet Willy or a wedgy at any time.

"Look out for falling rocks" signs are now abolished; it is not possible to drive and look for falling rocks at the same time.

Marijuana is now legal; however use of the phrases "Hey man" and "come on Dude" are now misdemeanors.

Deer will only be allowed to cross the highway where "Caution Deer Crossing" signs are posted.

Entry into our country now requires the understanding of "Exit", "Men's Room", "Lady's Room", "Slippery when wet", and "No smoking" signs.

Statutory rape by female teachers no longer applies to boys over 14. Statutory rape of an underage girl who has had breast implants is now only a misdemeanor.

All the above laws are irrevocable, and I am now stepping down to let the political process continue as we know it.

PHYSICS

Everyone knows all about $E=MC^2$, but what.........Ah I got nothing.

One last subject

FUNERALS

Obviously, no one likes funerals, but they are important rituals to mourn your loved one and put your grief to rest along with the deceased.

The rituals of funerals differ according to different cultures. Jews follow very strict rules during burials, followed by seven days of mourning (Shiva) at home. I did some research on Shiva and found the following:

It is customary during Shiva in order to focus complete attention on one's grief:

- sit low as a symbol of "being brought low" in grief.
- no "luxurious" bathing or cutting hair. These are signs of vanity.
- remove leather shoes and wear cloth slippers or sandals.
- covering mirrors for the same reason as not bathing.
- sexual relations are forbidden.
- mourners should not transact business.
- mourners may clean and cook for themselves.
- wherever possible morning and evening services should be held in the home.

Islam has similarly strict burial rules, followed by three days of mourning where I found the following:

Grief at the death of a beloved person is normal, and weeping for the dead (by males or females) is perfectly acceptable in Islam..

Islam does expect expression of one's grief to remain dignified: Islam prohibits the expression of grief by loud wailing (bewailing refers to mourning in a loud voice), shrieking, beating the chest and cheeks, tearing hair or clothes, breaking objects, scratching faces or speaking phrases that make a Muslim lose faith, although much is granted in practice as fatigue and emotion can adversely affect ones' behaviors, and such behavior is rarely censured.

I am not sure how Atheists mourn their dead, I guess they just say bye. "Not going to see ya, don't wanna be ya!"

Black people tend to make a dramatic show of their grief, shrieking, crying and sometimes even throwing themselves on the casket until they are forcibly pulled away. This is expected behavior.

White Protestants would frown on this, as a simple dabbing of the eyes with a tissue is their proper response.

The Irish celebrate their loved ones going to Heaven, and consumption of alcohol at wakes is well documented.

One common denominator to all cultures, I suspect, is the story telling and remembrances of all the great qualities of the deceased. These speeches are always very touching. It is a shame that the loved one did not hear how great they were while they were still alive.

I would like to have my funeral service before I die. Just sit at the head of the church and drink in all the accolades of how smart, fun, funny and loved I was (am). It is just something I don't want to miss.

For my actual funeral, I request that Matt secretly plant one of his remote controlled fart machines in the casket. At the most reverent moment, he should press the button for a Lord Windisphere triple woopsie sizzler!

My funeral will not soon be forgotten!

OK, it is DEFINITLY just me.